CW00515839

STEP-PARENTS,

Step-by-step

CHRISTINA HUGHES

KYLE CATHIE LIMITED

First published in Great Britain in 1993 by
Kyle Cathie Limited
7/8 Hatherley Street, London SW1P 2QT

ISBN 1 85626 082 8

A Cataloguing in Publication record for this title is
available from the British Library.

Typeset by DP Photosetting, Aylesbury, Bucks
Printed by Clays Ltd, Bungay, Suffolk

CONTENTS

FOR MY MUM AND IN MEMORY OF MY DAD

ACKNOWLEDGEMENTS

Writing a book is such a personal venture. So much of
yourself is captured in the printed page which seems to
have a life beyond your own. Writing a book also takes
over your life in every degree. The time in front of the PC
and the waking hours spent thinking about it are very
tangible signs of the intrusion of writing. Putting my six-
year-old daughter to bed, I play out sentences in my mind;
cooking the dinner, I work through ideas and themes; before
I finally fall asleep, the next chapter appears to haunt me. The
result of all this activity is that you cease to be available to
those around you. You may be physically sitting in the living-
room surrounded by your family but in your head you're in
the middle of Chapter Four debating the adequacy of the
pages you've written that day. It seems to me, therefore, that
whilst it's an incredibly hard job writing a book, it's possibly
even harder having to live with someone who is. For that
reason, I have to thank my husband, Steven Walker, who has
been a tower of strength throughout the past few months. Not
only has he listened and talked through with me the contents
of this book, he also took over the running of the house and
the care of our children. Without him, I doubt I would have
survived.

I must also thank all the stepparents who have so willingly
shared their experiences with me. I cannot thank them
enough for their generosity in allowing my own insight to
develop through their lives. My appreciation must also be

recorded for the way that my publisher, Kyle Cathie, has so gently encouraged me to complete this task. Her professionalism has been wonderful to work with.

Finally, I must thank my children, who each in their way have contributed to this book. Thank you, Siobhan, Nolan and Hannah for being there.

Christina Hughes
April 1993

1

WICKED, WICKED, WICKED STEPFAMILIES

'I thought I was the only one to feel this way.' Have you said those words? Did you think you were the only one who had bad thoughts about your stepchildren? Or couldn't cope with your stepfamily? If there is one message that I hope this book conveys it is to say that you are not alone. Reading this book may be the first step to finding out that your thoughts and feelings are shared by many, many stepparents. I can promise you they are. Let me start your journey of discovery by showing you how normal your circumstances are.

HOW NORMAL IS YOUR STEPFAMILY?

One way of looking at normality is to think of how many people live in stepfamilies. You may be surprised by the numbers. It is almost a commonplace to say that around one-third of all marriages now end in divorce. The riskiest time is the eighth year of marriage when most divorces occur. One marriage in three is also a remarriage. There are about 120,000 remarriages each year, the most usual being between a divorced man and a divorced woman. Over half of women who divorce are remarried within six years. There are no clear statistics telling us the exact numbers of children living in stepfamilies but it is estimated that around one child in ten is being brought up in a stepfamily. All in all that is an awful lot of people.

Another way of looking at the normality of stepfamily life

is to reflect for a moment on the rich and famous who are stepparents or stepchildren: Yoko Ono, much publicised stepmother of Julian Lennon; Jerry Hall, in a similar situation with Mick Jagger's children. Then there are the British royal steprelations. Through her second marriage, Princess Anne's children have acquired a stepfather. Both Diana, the Princess of Wales, and Sarah, the Duchess of York, have stepparents as the consequence of the divorces of their parents. Indeed, it is likely that Diana and Sarah could well become stepmothers themselves if they remarry. Their remarriages would certainly lead to their children acquiring stepfathers. The same may be true of Princes Charles and Andrew whose remarriages would certainly give their children stepmothers and who may also themselves become stepfathers. One wonders if the era of the stepfamily has finally arrived through the 'By Appointment' seal of royal approval?

When I think of my own family I begin to realise how surrounded we are by the normality of remarriage. In addition to my own situation as a stepmother, my husband is also a stepfather to our eldest stepdaughter. My two brothers-in-law also divorced and one, before his untimely death, became a stepfather. His first wife also remarried and my nephews have a stepfather. My other brother-in-law's children have a stepmother who looks after them full-time and a stepfather who lives with their non-custodial mother. My sister, similarly divorced and remarried, acquired a stepfather for her son. Finally, my father-in-law, in his 70s, remarried after a long period as a widower and I acquired a wonderful stepmother-in-law. The complexity of family relationships is not only confined to my family and the royal family, I hasten to add. The man who sells us our insurance is a stepfather, his wife a stepmother. The children of the chap who came to plaster our bedroom ceilings have just acquired a stepfather. Three families of the eight living near us are stepfamilies. And I haven't begun to count the close friends who are in a similar situation. If you feel you are alone, just begin to think of all the people you form. Any other type is seen to be less than perfect. The stepfamily is not the only family to face this problem. All families which do not conform to the ideal type are equally seen as inferior. This inferiority spans families brought up by a lone parent to those headed by lesbian and gay couples. Even class and racial issues rear their heads here as the basis for comparison. The stepfamily is, therefore, not alone in its inferior status.

Why does society continue to hold the traditional family in such high esteem? One important reason is because of the role of the family in bringing up children. It is here that the ideal family of two parents plus children is invested with almost magical powers. And because the stepfamily is less than perfect, people consequently think that it must cause problems for its children.

'CHILDREN COME FIRST'

We place a lot of emphasis in our society on the needs of our children. Children come first. It's as simple as that. This focus is confirmed by Penelope Leach in her book *Baby and Child*. The first words she writes in her introduction to this book are '*Baby and Child* is written from your baby or child's point of view because, however fashion in child-rearing may shift and alter, that viewpoint is both the most important and the most neglected.' The idea that children's needs come first has also been supported through the work of child psychologists. In particular, they have said that children can suffer emotional damage if they are separated from their parents. Children's psychologists such as John Bowlby are part of the army of experts who promulgate this view. Writing in the 1950s and 1960s Bowlby warned of the dire consequences for children separated too early from their mother. He said such children would be psychologically damaged by this lack of mother-love. The result? Guilt and contrition placed on the shoulders of any mother who dares go out to work and leave her child in the care of another.

Children's needs have also been transposed into children's

rights. Charities in England such as ChildLine gives children access to help in an independent way and gives them a chance to circumvent adult control. Perhaps the most telling area of children's rights is the fact that children can now 'divorce' their parents if they don't come up to standard. More recently, in Britain one teenage boy was taking his mother to the High Court because she had refused to visit him. Under British law he has a right of access to his mother – whether she wanted it or not. Children are gaining a voice that hitherto has been denied them.

How does this emphasis on the child affect the stepfamily? There are several issues that need to be considered:

- Divorce suggests you are already a bad parent because you would not have got divorced if you had put your children's needs first;
- Children in stepfamilies have already been damaged by divorce or loss and so it is a harder parenting task;
- Can stepparents be unselfish enough to put their step-children's needs first?

Whilst the first family is seen to provide the ideal structure in which to raise children, as we have seen, the stepfamily is not viewed in this way. True, there are two parents plus children but somehow the damage caused to children through their parents' marriage breakdown places the stepfamily in a position of having to do a lot of repair work. Can it do it? Worse still, at least one parent has singularly failed to put their children first. They are already failures as parents, as their failed marriage proves. Not a very auspicious start to the task of repairing damaged children, is it? the critics say.

As I've said, the stepfamily is not alone in being seen to be somehow an inferior family form. This is important to know because it means that we can get this supposed inferiority into perspective. We are in a no-win situation. Think about society's attitude to lone-parent families. Usually headed by mothers, they are also seen to be inadequate to the task of bringing up children properly. They mostly lack, it is thought, the firmness or role model offered by a father.

Lesbian and gay families are seen to be even more outrageous. It is thought they give children quite the wrong ideas about sexuality and appropriate partners. Diversity, as far as families are concerned, is not a cause for celebration.

Within these ideas there is what we might call a contamination theory. That is, that by being brought up in these supposedly inferior family forms, these children will themselves become single parents, gay or lesbian, even, heaven forbid, for those brought up in a stepfamily, stepparents. In other words, they will be damaged in some sort of way.

Whilst the natural parent has failed as a parent by ending up in a stepfamily, stepparents have the same requirements placed upon them as if they were natural parents. They too are expected to put their stepchildren first. In this respect they are seen to be no different from natural parents. As stepparents we are asked to put our own needs and feelings last. The stepchild comes first. Can stepparents do this? No more or less than a natural parent is my guess. Yet there is a difference. The steprelationship looks for some reward for its hard work. Without the bond with the child that natural parents may have, and the automatic assumption that there is mutual love, putting others first is not an easy option. Think of it this way. Would you find it easy to put the needs of your neighbours' children before your own needs? Would you buy your neighbours' child a new dress when you haven't had one yourself for six months? Especially if you didn't like them that much? This is close to what can be asked of stepparents.

However, because it is an expectation of natural parents, stepparents take on the same expectation for themselves. They want to be good parents. When they fail, as inevitably they sometimes do, their self-esteem crumbles. In reality, they haven't failed the stepparent test, they've failed the parent test. But because the two roles are so intertwined it gets very difficult to disentangle them.

However, as a second-class family type, the stepfamily has one advantage over other 'abnormal' families. It is invisible to the outside eye. This takes us into the next stage of understanding the stepfamily. Stepfamilies can pass as 'normal' families. The stigma that its members feel gives them the dilemma of whether or not they should do so.

THE STEPFAMILY: A CLOSETED FAMILY?

Many books on the stepfamily start by giving a definition of the stepfamily. One definition would be that it includes two partners, at least one of whom brings children from a previous relationship to the family. This may either be full-time, when the children live permanently with the couple, or part-time, when children visit at weekends or holidays. However, as a variant of the family, the stepfamily is also hidden from view. The stepfamily recreates, at least in outward appearances, the ideal family – two parents plus children, living in one unit.

It has been suggested that the stepfamily solves many of the problems society sees in the lone-parent family. With two parents in the family unit, all the financial and emotional support families need are met. Society can breathe a sigh of relief and forget all about it. Stepfamily members therefore live in a family which is neither approved of by society, yet not quite so vilified either. Yet this very ambiguity means that they sit uneasily in the closet, unsure of whether to disclose they are living in a stepfamily or to keep quiet about it. This raises its own problems:

● Do you publicly own up to living in a stepfamily and risk all the negative associations that people hold about step-families being channelled at your family?
● Do you keep quiet and live a lie, causing confusion and reinforcing the invisibility of the stepfamily?

Because of the negative undertones associated with the stepfamily, to speak out and talk of the problems of living in this type of family may only confirm the public image. To say nothing leaves one alone to sort problems out without support. At a more personal level, owning up that your children are stepchildren, or your parent is a stepparent, immediately opens up your past history. You haven't managed to live up to the ideal. There is an internal sense of disadvantage – an inferiority complex which becomes public knowledge. At your stepchild's school parents' evening you have to go into a long rigmarole of explanation about your exact relationship to the child. The teacher benignly smiles and singles out your child as facing potential problems. How many of you have felt this kind of public disapproval which leads to the likelihood that your stepchild's behaviour or aptitudes will be viewed in a particular way?

Whilst remarriage might therefore solve some of the more undesirable features of living alone – poverty, loneliness, bringing up children with no adult support – it also brings with it its unique problems. Living in the closet, you know you haven't escaped completely the associations connected to your past. The continuing power of the ideal family will continue to rear its head and roar at you to remind you that you have failed in some way to live up to expectations. It is, at times, an uncomfortable existence owning a stepfamily. Moreover, there is always the nagging fear that these negative ideas have some basis in fact.

Is the Stepfamily Bad for its Members?

Not only does the stepfamily have to live in the shadow of the ideal family form, it can also be viewed as a maelstrom of discord. We hear a lot about the problems between stepparents and stepchildren and between ex-partners and the new family. We hear that stepchildren may leave school earlier, gain fewer qualifications and themselves end up in broken marriages. We hear that one-third of all remarriages end in divorce, indicating that we cannot even get it right second time around, or indicating that it is so difficult living in a stepfamily many rapidly give up. Let us look at the evidence that suggests stepfamilies are problem families. These include:

- the growth of counselling and advice organisations;
- turning everyday events into crises;

- research that looks for problems to solve;
- pathologising all responses to divorce and remarriage.

The growing number of books devoted to helping people cope with stepfamily life – of which this book is one! – indicates the growing interest here. The formation of organisations to help stepfamilies suggests that support is needed for potential difficulties. In addition, conciliation services, marriage guidance counsellors and so forth all exist because of the problems of family and stepfamily living. It is not surprising that with all this activity we tend to hear a lot about the problems of the stepfamily rather than the benefits.

Is the stepfamily truly the vipers' nest of acrimony that popular imagination would have us believe? I don't think so. Again I think it's a question of getting things into perspective. True, there can be a lot of bad feeling in the stepfamily. But so is there in any family. Unfortunately, as we've seen, stepfamilies start out from a position of disadvantage because of their supposed inferiority. Add to this that in stepfamily relationships the normal cut and thrust of family life seems to be magnified out of proportion and stepparents rapidly feel vulnerable from all directions. Many children tell their parents they hate them. We know they don't. And they know we still love them despite how they behave. For a stepparent to be told 'I hate you', though, is taken at its face value. The stepparent believes it. It fulfils our innermost fear that we are unlovable. Indeed, given the guilt we carry about our less-than-perfect stepparenting and the less-than-perfect family form we inhabit, we can almost believe the statement is justified.

Researchers, and I include myself here also, are just as bad at focusing on the problematic features of a situation. Just like the media, I suspect, where bad news is the news, researchers look for problems to solve. In that sense, therefore, research can contribute to the poor images we carry of divorce and remarriage. Research asks questions like 'Is divorce bad for children?' or 'What are the problems of stepparenting?' In so doing, we may be reinforcing the notion that each of these states is a problem rather than a blessing.

Further, professionals concerned with the family can turn even positive responses to life changes into problems. Helen Franks, in her book *Remarriage*, takes issue with the way that therapists, marriage guidance counsellors and sociologists view the maintenance of good relationships between spouses after divorce as pathological. It seems you can't win either way! On the one hand, divorced parents are berated if they criticise the absent parent, row in front of the children, and generally act as enemies. To act in these ways is to undermine your child's security, to create loyalty problems and to make it difficult for your child to travel between two new worlds.

On the other hand, those who continue – in .the best interests of their children don't forget – in amicable relationships, who continue to share outings with their children, and behave as 'mature adults', are likely to encourage the fantasy every child supposedly believes, that their parents are going to get back together. Unfair on the kids, the experts say. And, moreover, how can the child understand the reason why you have broken up in the first place if you continue to appear as if you like each other? So, you mustn't appear to hate your ex but you mustn't appear to like her/him either. Give us a break.

Is it any wonder that we continue to believe that essentially any deviation from the ideal is unworkable, given the conflict in the advice given? That somehow the stepfamily must be bad for its members? If those parents who follow the experts' advice to its logical end are getting it wrong, what about us lesser mortals? We are in another no-win situation.

All this suggests that stepfamilies start out with the odds stacked against them through the kinds of attitudes that society brings to bear on them. Stepfamily members are almost in the position of having to do a lot of public relations work to overcome some of this inbuilt antagonism in the system. Should we therefore continue to believe that our problems are solely the result of our own inadequacies?

ASKING THE INDIVIDUAL TO CHANGE THEIR BEHAVIOUR

Did you feel a sense of personal blame when your marriage broke up or when your stepchild packed her bags and left home? Did you think the reason for this was because you as an individual are not very good at making relationships work? I would not be surprised if you did. But have you ever asked where these ideas come from? Here is one example. One of the very powerful ideas underpinning family therapy is the notion that we are continually recreating the same problems in our personal relationships. If we got it wrong first time around, we are likely to get it wrong second and third and fourth, and so on – until we change our behaviour. Where does the basis of our behaviour come from? The answer, at bottom, is from our parents. We unconsciously learn from the way our parents behave towards each other that this is the way to live our own lives.

The patterns and behaviours which we grew up with, the argument goes, are those that we automatically look for in others. We choose someone as a partner who fits the bill in this kind of way. Unfortunately, if our parents had some kind of problem in their relationship we will also have the same kind of problems because we are in a cycle of choosing to make relationships with people who remind us of the way we were brought up.

An extract from Sarah Litvinoff's book, *The Relate Guide to Starting Again*, illustrates this. And my apologies to Sarah for putting the spotlight on her work in this way. It is not meant to criticise unjustly what is undeniably a good book. Rather I want to bring out the difference between various understandings of how families work. Sarah Litvinoff makes the following comments under the title 'What attracted you to each other in the first place?':

The most important point to remember when you attempt to understand what drew you both together, is that your choice of partner depends on the sort of person you are. And that, in turn, depends on your experiences while you were growing up. Often, what

seems so 'right' about your partner are ways of behaving and emotional reactions that are familiar to you,
because in some ways they remind you of the inter-
actions in your own family. This can be the case even if
those ways of behaving didn't make you happy in the
past. You know where you are with them.

But hang on. OK, I'm looking for familiarity. So I'm looking
for someone who behaves in the same way as my family did.
But the argument then goes on to put us in that no-win
situation again. If I happen to find someone who is different
that isn't going to be any good either. As Sarah Litvinoff goes
on to say:

However you can also be drawn to someone who
behaves in very different ways from what you have
experienced in your family, because you hope to be
different yourself. Sometimes this very difference,
initially attractive, causes you problems in the end.
Perhaps your partner had qualities that you admired,
and would like to have had yourself.

As a non-expert in this field I would be the last to say that the
ideas are wrong. But I do have several problems with them.
Turning all our behaviours into problems is one.

Another is that it focuses so much on the individual that if
it's not blaming you, it's blaming your parents. If your
parents had behaved towards each other in appropriate
ways, had dealt with their anger and confrontations in
appropriate ways, had shown love and kindness in appropriate ways, all would be well. This view tells you that your
parents have not shown you how to create a healthy close
relationship. By implication it's telling you that if you now
don't create 'healthy close relationships' your children will be
similarly damaged. Collective guilt all round.

What I sincerely believe to be a problem with this kind of
work is the focus it places on the individual to change. What
about changing some of the structures in which we live and
some of the expectations we have of people, rather than

blaming the individual for their problems as if they were personal failings? I wouldn't want to throw out of the window all the scholarship that has gone into developing family therapy and similar approaches. However, I would like to add something equally important to it.

AN ALTERNATIVE VIEW?

You could say that I too am biased towards seeing and understanding the world in a certain kind of way. In particular I tend to look at the way society defines and shapes people's lives. Within families, one significant example is the roles women and men have. Very simply, women are carers, men are breadwinners. I do not say this is the way family life ought to be. Indeed, this is an area where many, including myself, would like to see widespread change. However, there is a tendency in our society to attribute caring roles to women, breadwinner roles to men. Women grow up thinking their main role in life is to be a wife and mother. Men grow up with the notion that to fulfil their breadwinner role they will be in paid work for life. Our gender role therefore has a strong influence on our experiences.

From this viewpoint we can even predict the likely choices that women and men will make in their lives. Let us consider a very obvious example of work and career. Here we know, by looking at statistics, and indeed from our own experience, that the majority of women take a break from work when they have children. They return part-time when their children reach school age, often to a less qualified job than the one they had before their children came along, in order to fit work around the needs of children and school. Men may be forced, through redundancy and unemployment, to take a break but will not automatically expect to do so on the birth of their children.

In this way, we can see how features of social life affect the way we behave and the way we view the world. These perceptions of our roles affect the choices that we make for ourselves or are allowed to make. It is a view that argues that we do not have the complete free choice in our lives that outward appearances of the world might suggest.

Let us return to Sarah Litvinoff's book to illustrate this further. Sarah Litvinoff gives an example of the way 'influences from the past' operate on our unconscious choice of a partner through this case history:

Mandy had a domineering father and a mother who did everything in the home and sheltered behind her husband. Mandy was her father's pet. She was pretty, clever and capable and she could do no wrong in her father's eyes. Mandy had despised her mother as a child and didn't want to be like her. Now at thirty-five Mandy was close to her mother and saw things differently. She saw that her mother had been unhappy for many years, but had been too weak to assert herself.

What this meant was that Mandy had no idea how a healthy, close and balanced relationship operated.

The family therapy explanation takes account of the fact that many women 'do everything for men' as in the case of Mandy's mother. The need for change however must come from Mandy – though where this leaves her partner's responsibility for making the relationship work is unclear. Mandy must learn that she is repeating the patterns of her parents' relationship in her own. Once she has become 'conscious' of this, she has the power to change the pattern of her relationships.

Another explanation is indeed that the vast majority of women are brought up to 'do everything for men'. It is part of the way our society orders its family, as I have outlined above. In this view Mandy's parents were not therefore pathological in any sense. They were not bad parents. They were simply replicating the roles of an ideal family. Asking Mandy to change her behaviour in this context is a bit like asking the *Titanic* not to sink. Without also seeking some kind of wider change in the way we see the appropriate roles for women and men in families, Mandy is very much swimming against the tide. I would go so far as to say that, whilst some aspects of her behaviour may be modified through this knowledge, essentially all women are Mandys to some extent. It is not merely by their parents that they are schooled to be helpmates and carers. Schools until recently divided subjects according to sex – needlework and cookery for the girls, woodwork for the boys. Take a look at television advertising – particularly those soap powder adverts. How many men do you see who wouldn't swap their one packet for two? It is all too easy to blame parents, as it is stepparents, for our problems rather than seeing that some of our problems arise from the way we organise our lives.

IT'S NOT ME, IT'S THE SITUATION

Now let me briefly show you how you can use this knowledge to improve your own stepfamily life. In this book I shall ask you to consider some of the features of your life that you take for granted. Who changes the bed linen, for example? By asking even the simplest questions, my aim is to make you consider this: that the way your life is constructed – both by yourself and by the expectations placed upon you – is the reason for some of the difficulties you face as a stepparent.

As I've said, my aim is that this book should act as a counterbalance to the most prominent reason why we think we face difficulties – that as individual stepparents we are failures. The book emphasises that the problems are not you, they are most often the result of the situation you are in. Focusing on the situation not self is the start of the liberating process. Too often stepparents are dogged with personal feelings of inadequacy. This leads to a loss of self-esteem and a downward spiral of self-hate – hardly the basis on which to build healthy relationships. Similarly, stepparents live with a nagging sense of injustice. While we all agree life is not fair, for stepparents there are many features of double injustice. It's hard enough working bringing up your own children, with precious little thanks at the end of it, but bringing up other people's children with no reward and a lot of aggravation is doubly so.

One of the most liberating steps we can take is to find that we are not alone with our problems. Stepfamily groups not only give mutual support but the sharing of experiences says that our individual experiences are not unique. The most important step that I took as a stepmother was to read Brenda Maddox's book *The Half-Parent* (now reprinted as *Stepparenting*). You cannot imagine how wonderful it felt to read about the lives of other stepmothers and to know that I was not alone in the feelings I had. It was a turning point for me and I began to see that perhaps I wasn't so bad as I thought I was. It gave me the ability to look at things a little more objectively.

One of the stepmothers in my research study used to show her husband the letters in the *Stepfamily Newsletter* with the comment 'I didn't write it'. These letters told the same stories, expressed the same feelings, that she was experiencing. She felt her husband treated her as if she was slightly neurotic. He shrugged off her feelings and told her she was 'going over the top'. By showing him the letters it was her way of saying 'It's not me, it's the situation'.

I hope that one thing you can learn from this book is to say to yourself 'It's not me, it's the situation' and that this phrase will help to create some distance between you and the problems you are facing. I hope it will help you to stop blaming yourself unjustly.

What I don't want you to do, however, is to end up blaming someone else! With this in mind let's look at some of the internal dynamics of stepfamilies.

THE TRILOGY OF WICKEDNESS

Open any book on the stepfamily and you will find the tales of Cinderella and Snow White. You will find mention, often very frequent mention, of the wicked stepmother. This book is no different. As Donna Smith in *Stepmother* comments, 'Now, as in the past, stepmothers have to contend with the image of the "wicked stepmother".' Yet in some books on the stepfamily there is evident irritation at the amount of attention this warrants. Thus, Stephen Collins in *Stepparents and their Children* chides us that 'myths have no place in the modern stepfamily'. Whilst I would agree that myths should not have such a place and would wish that surely to God we have gone beyond the power of ancient storytelling, evidently, by the amount of attention stepparents themselves give to ideas of wickedness, we have not. Stepparents in the 1990s still feel that they are facing all the negative associations of medieval fairy tales.

One of the most interesting features of my work on the stepfamily has been to understand the significance of the trilogy of wickedness. This trilogy consists of:

● the wicked stepmother
● the wicked stepchild
● the wicked ex-partner.

Let us look at each in turn.

THE WICKED STEPMOTHER

I read Cinderella to my daughter the other day, the 1985 version published by Ladybird. Let me give you some of the story in case you had forgotten it.

> Once upon a time, in a far away place, there lived a beautiful girl called Cinderella. She lived in an old house with her stepmother and two stepsisters. They were horrid to her because she was beautiful and they were not.
>
> ... But her cruel stepmother and stepsisters laughed at her. 'How can you go to the ball? You have nothing to wear. And anyway, you will have to help us to get ready,' they said.
>
> ... Cinderella came into the room. 'Oh!' he [the prince] said, turning to her stepmother. 'But I thought you said that there were no other girls in this house!'
>
> 'She's only a servant,' said the stepmother. 'She did not go to the ball!'

... The ugly sisters and the cruel stepmother were furious that Cinderella should have the other glass slipper.

Reading this story to my daughter I realised quite forcibly how strongly we still perpetuate these ideas to our children through the stories they hear. No wonder that many, many stepmothers feel they are seen by society as a modern wicked stepmother. We are still telling our children through their stories that we are! The wicked stepmother myth affects stepmothers in the following ways:

- it makes them fearful that, because they are a stepmother, any seemingly uncaring action they take will be seen by the world as evidence of their innate wickedness;
- the wicked stepmother is the opposite of the good mother. Stepmothers have to work harder to prove they are not wicked.

The effect of the Cinderella myth is that stepmothers feel that their every action will be judged on these terms. Just like the stepmother in the story, we will treat our stepchildren as servants. We will be jealous of their good looks. We will ensure they don't have a good time. We would certainly be profoundly upset if they made good in life and married the prince!

Stepmothers therefore feel hamstrung by the myth. If they do chide or chastise their stepchildren, the fingers will point. If they do confess that they don't like their stepchild, heads will nod knowingly. The myth is like a big label saying:

Watch how this person behaves: she is likely to be very nasty indeed.

The stepmothers in my own research had developed a range of strategies to combat the myth, some of which we consider in Chapter Two. They would avoid confrontation with stepchildren, for example, or be extra nice – neither of which changes the myth itself, but at least they enable stepmothers to avoid the stigma.

Another way of looking at the wicked stepmother myth is as an opposite. Stepmothers are bad. Mothers are good. Why we should imbue stepmothers with all the bad properties of mothering is open to question. Psychologists talk of 'splitting theories' where the child splits the good mother – that is his or her natural mother – away from the bad mother – you've guessed it, the stepmother. It's a thought.

Whatever the reason, to understand being a stepmother we have to know that they face these negative connotations of being inevitably a bad mother. This is something which many women find very hard to come to terms with. Women, as I've discussed, are brought up to see themselves as nurturers and carers. There is a lot of significance attached to being a good mother in our society. To be thought of as a bad one is a raw deal indeed. This is why stepmothers go to such great lengths to avoid being seen to be nasty. They become superstep-mums, breaking their backs to prove they are worthy. It is that, or be strong enough to swim against the tide.

The Wicked Stepchild

Is it sacrilege to call a stepchild wicked? They are usually portrayed as the innocent victims of their parents' failures. Brenda Maddox, in her book *The Half-Parent*, has a chapter entitled 'The desolate stepchild', indicating the pathos attached to that state. Indeed, stepchildren are seen in two distinctly opposite ways:

- on the one hand, they are seen to be suffering as unloved children in a stepfamily;
- on the other hand, they are seen to be the cause of much stepparental suffering.

The findings of research which we consider in Chapter Four highlight the problems that stepchildren face in the stepfamily. It would appear from this research that there is indeed a degree of unhappiness among stepchildren of which we need to take significant account. One of the ways to do this is to begin to look at the problems from both sides – that is, from the stepparent's and from the stepchild's points of view. What appears to happen, however, is that we get a dominance of one view or the other. 'Look at how the stepchild feels,' shouts one corner. 'Look at how the stepparent feels,' shouts the other corner. I have therefore tried, in Chapter Four, to show both viewpoints by counterposing the two sides. The weight of responsibility in this book, however, given its focus, still lies with the adult – the price of age, I suspect, though I promise I won't tell you to be mature about your relationships! It's always struck me as a rather crass attitude, particularly when, as stepparents, we often don't feel very mature.

The notion of the wicked stepchild arose from my own research on stepparents. Many stepparents could indeed believe that their stepchild was, at times, pretty nasty. They would tell me that whilst they were doing their very best, their stepchild was behaving hatefully. I don't have any problem believing that. As one stepfather told me about his early stepfamily experiences: 'They were just horrible kids and kids are horrible anyway.' What we have to do, if ever we are going to change things, is to explore the factors that lead us to see children as wicked.

It is argued that stepparents expect more gratitude from their stepchildren than parents do from their natural children. I would probably want to turn this around a little and say that stepparents need extra signs that they are loved and wanted than do natural parents. There can be no automatic assumption that love is present between stepparent and stepchild. Both sides are constantly looking for signs.

One of the main findings of my research was the way that praise from a stepchild or the meagrest sign of affection was seized upon and valued intensely. The first words one stepmother said to me once, with evident joy, when I visited her was that her stepdaughter had told her she loved her. In my own case I remember my stepson buying balloons saying 'Happy Birthday Mum' for me when I married his father on mine (and his father's!) birthday. He told me it was his sign of accepting me. Indeed it was. It was the most wonderfully thoughtful and loving gesture. All the struggles of the past seven years, and the next ten, were made worthwhile in that moment.

I am not surprised that those stepparents who do not receive such signs see their job as little more than being an unthanked workhorse. The ensuing resentment is exacerbated by all those nasty little moments when your stepchild tells you a lie, or shows distaste at your presence. It is heightened when your stepchild tells you how wonderful his or her mother is or what a clever dad she or he has. It is aggravated by a feeling that your stepchild could be deceitful or has cast him or herself in the role of Cinderella/Cinderfella. And all these moments add up. They become a string of stories which you can recount, one by one, to support your view of what a disagreeable little toerag your stepchild is.

When this happens you have in fact created a myth about them. The story of Cinderella sets out a series of incidents to show how wicked her stepmother was – treating Cinderella as a servant, being jealous of her beauty, trying to stop her going to the ball. All these incidents add up to confirmation of how evil the stepmother was. In just the same way, we as stepparents can build up a series of stories about our stepchildren which focus on their worst (or best) behaviour.

The pattern of the myth is incredibly difficult to break. It sets out a series of statements that support all the reasons why this person is so unlikeable. As we shall see, it is not just stepchildren about whom myths are made. The ex-partner is also someone about whom we can tell a few tales.

THE WICKED EX-PARTNER

Divorce or widowhood may signal the official end of a marriage but, as many second wives and husbands will confirm, become someone's second or third partner and you'll quickly find you haven't just married them. You've married your new partner's ex as well. Whether divorced or widowed, the ex continues to exert a presence over the stepfamily that does not disappear, wish it as you might.

There is one major reason why the ex exerts a presence in your life – the children, of course. For the divorced, access and maintenance are tangible ties that bind a previous partner to you. For the widowed, the sense of following in someone's footsteps in the parenting of their children can be just as tangible. To put it mildly, the ex can be irksome company. There is much debate about which state is the most irksome however. It is played out in terms of the ghost versus the reality of the non-custodial parent.

We assume that marriages which end with the death of a spouse were happy and fulfilling. Following in the footsteps of someone whom you perceive as much loved is a very different experience to marrying someone who has been through the trauma of the divorce process. Will they continue to burn a candle in their heart for them? Ever-fallible in real life, how can you compete with a ghost? One real constraint faced is that it is very difficult to be critical. As we know, one mustn't speak ill of the dead. The idealised version of the deceased parent is accordingly one that you cannot challenge very easily, at least, not without appearing distinctly unfeeling. In my experience, therefore, stepparents in this situation do not perceive the deceased partner as malicious or spiteful. At least, if they do, they are not allowed to say so publicly. This is not the case however with the divorced.

Brenda Maddox speaks of the tales she heard about previous partners. 'She was hallucinating. They lived in filth.' 'He was alcoholic – out of the picture for long stretches.' 'She runs up these fantastic bills and tells the children that he isn't giving her enough to support them.' So the stories go on. I could add my own here about my partner's ex-wife. I do not know anyone married to a divorced person who hasn't got such tales to tell. The existence of these stories begs the question, have all our partners previously married hateful people? I doubt it. There must have been some mutual love at some stage in the relationship. So why do so many of us feel outraged by the ex's behaviour? I think the answer lies firstly in the continuing financial and organisational dependence which children of divorce create. Secondly, the antagonism is fuelled by the adversarial nature of the divorce process. Thirdly, there is the control that an ex still continues to have in your life. These are all issues we consider in this book.

THE STEPFATHER

You may have noticed that so far the stepfather has escaped the attribution of wickedness which is placed on almost every other relationship in the stepfamily. Personally, I find this extremely unfair! Indeed, the stepfather is often viewed as a saviour, come to rescue a poor mother and her children from distress. 'What a good chap,' friends murmur quietly, 'to take on all that.'

The stepfather can nevertheless find himself with his own unique problems. In particular, he can find that he is both a stepfather to someone else's children and a non-custodial father of his own. Although there is less stigma attached to men who leave their families than to women who leave theirs, the stepfather can feel guilt about his absence from his own children which may be mixed up with a sense of responsibility for his stepchildren. The expectations placed on men to be providers can also place particular pressures on the stepfather, especially if he has continuing maintenance to pay to his first family. All in all, therefore, being a stepfather can be a tricky balancing act. How you maintain the balance is the subject of Chapter Three.

REVIEW

The key messages of this chapter are:

- there are thousands of stepfamilies, your situation is not unique;
- the problems people see in stepfamilies give you troubles before you start;
- rather than blaming yourself, consider life in relation to what is expected of any parent;
- understanding is the key to success.

Remember: You are not alone.

2

SUPERHEROINES

Being a stepmother is the toughest job in the world. You know this. You experience it every day. What you may not know is that there is a wealth of research which confirms your experience. There is no doubt, therefore, that your journey through stepmotherhood will be hard and demanding. It will ask things of you you don't want to give. It will at times be, and probably has already been, sheer hell. BUT ... it can also be challenging, rewarding and successful. My aim in this chapter is to show you how you can be a success as a stepmother, and how you can feel more able to cope with the many facets of your life.

I'm not promising that this will be easy. Fundamentally, I am going to ask you to examine many aspects of your life:

- from the physical activities you do every day ...
- to those feelings of responsibility stepmothers have about their stepchildren;
- from how being a stepmother can lead to guilt and low self-esteem ...
- to some practical ways of coping with that age-old, but very prevalent, wicked stepmother myth.

You should be aware, however, that underlying all this activity is one principal idea. Whilst there are some aspects of being a stepmother which are unique, overall the roles, responsibilities and expectations placed on stepmothers overlap with those of being female and being a mother. To make stepmothering successful, therefore, you need to understand the way being a stepmother in our society is linked to being both a woman and a mother. This is where I think most advice books on the stepfamily have got it wrong. They focus on the 'special' features of stepfamily life rather than having a broader conception that a major constituent of the job of being a stepmother is that of mothering. And mothering is something associated with being female.

However, there is one unique feature of being a stepmother which appears to play a large part in the way we handle this role. That is, the wicked stepmother myth. This myth defines the nature of the stepmother job. It gives it an extremely negative image. Unfortunately it is that negative image that stepmothers have to negotiate every day. Nevertheless, even the wicked stepmother myth can be linked quite clearly to images about mothers. As we saw in the last chapter, they are opposites. Whilst mothers are imbued with the positive features of nurturing and caring; stepmothers are evil and nasty: the good mother; the bad stepmother.

Remember: Stepmothers and mothers are seen to be opposite sides of the same coin.

In looking at ways that stepmothers can improve their lives, this chapter asks three main questions:

- Why do stepmothers have the hardest job?
- What is expected of stepmothers in their mothering role?
- How do the distinctive experiences of being a stepmother affect women's lives?

WHY DO STEPMOTHERS HAVE THE HARDEST JOB?

'My advice to other stepmothers? Don't do it. If I'd known what it was really like I don't think I would have married Jeff, no matter how much I cared about him. It's all been just awful.'

This stepmother's words are typical of those I hear all the time when I talk to women who have taken on the job of stepmother. Loving a man is no recompense for bringing up his children. Why, we must ask, is it just so awful? Research suggests that the problems stepmothers encounter are connected to:

- the extent of their previous experience with children generally;
- children's experience of being in a lone-parent family before acquiring a stepmother;
- expectations of being a good mother;
- the bad image of stepmotherhood.

Our first step therefore is to examine these a little more.

AND WHAT PREVIOUS EXPERIENCE AS A WIFE AND MOTHER HAVE YOU HAD?

Statistics indicate that a large proportion of stepmothers are women who were previously childless and unmarried. This suggests that such women have less experience both at being part of a couple and at looking after children than their previously married counterparts; and that they have to make greater adjustments to their new status.

Although I was divorced, as a childless, newly single woman, this was certainly the category I fitted into. I entered into the state of stepmotherhood with absolutely no prior experience of bringing up children. In fact, at the time I would not have described myself as the motherly type. Children just did not figure in my life. You can imagine the adjustments I therefore had to make to my lifestyle. The spontaneous nature of single life was replaced by the need to plan and to arrange babysitters. Money was very tight. My life became very restricted in all kinds of ways. If this wasn't bad enough, I was shocked at the amount of physical hard work and emotional toil being a stepmother involved. My memories of those early days are of endless washing, ironing and cleaning. What I didn't know was how normal this amount of work was in families with children.

How Damaged Are Your Stepchildren?

Not only do stepmothers have to contend with the physical aspects of caring for children, but they take on children who have experienced disruption and unhappiness in their short lives. For children who lose their mothers, whether through death or divorce, this is seen to be harder than losing a father. This is because we see mothers as being at the heart of the family; they are the ones that do all the caring and looking after. We also consider that the relationship between a mother and her child is absolutely essential to the child's all-round development.

We can see elements of this all around us. For example, ideas that mothers with young children should not go out to work or the kids will become delinquents or maladjusted.

When children lose their mother, it is believed that they experience more disruption than when they lose their father. Who is going to care for them? Who is going to do the cooking and cleaning? Who is going to be there after school? These features of everyday life become problems to be overcome by the father, who may also have a job to go to and who doesn't have the necessary housewifely skills. Children may experience a series of temporary, living-on-the-hoof arrangements. Some children find ways of coping by trying to replace the absent mother. We all know how a child can become the 'little mother' of the house.

For the incoming stepmother, these children's experiences can make it a more difficult job. They may be more stressed, or conversely they may have grown more used to having quite a lot of freedom, given the absence of the father, earning a living.

This was indeed the situation encountered by one stepmother I know. Her new partner had become widowed suddenly and he struggled with a job which required him to work unsocial hours as well as bringing up two teenage boys. The children, this stepmother described, became more wild in their behaviour, to the extent of breaking doors and windows to get into the house and being on the street till late at night. Neighbours began to complain about their behaviour. After the initial help from family and friends had dissipated, the father was left with a series of ad-hoc arrangements to provide a necessary adult presence whilst he was at work. Enter the stepmother. Her job was to create order from chaos. Clearly welcomed by the father as a saviour of his life, this was not how his children viewed it. As we would suspect, imposing discipline on two errant teenage boys can be an impossible task.

How Good a Mother are You?

To understand the expectations placed on stepmothers we must begin with what it means to be a mother. In her book, *Stepmothering*, Donna Smith says, 'Society puts stepmothers in the same hallowed place as "mothers".' In other words, society expects the same behaviour from a stepmother as it does from a mother.

In our sophisticated society, social rules for parental behaviour are often not made explicit in the same way as rules for, say, being a school-pupil or being a paid worker. In these cases, establishments place various expectations on the individual – for example, being punctual and working hard. There are, indeed, very strict rules about how we should behave as mothers and therefore as stepmothers, but they are hidden and unwritten. And because they are hidden, and can be incredibly subtle, it is often not easy to see how social rules of behaviour apply until they are broken.

There have been some recent examples reported in the press about the behaviour of the British royal mothers which have certainly been viewed as unacceptable as good motherly conduct. For example, the Duchess of York was photographed topless with a male friend. Princess Diana did not spend Christmas Day with her children. Even the Queen's motherly behaviour has come under scrutiny and she has been blamed for the relationship problems that Prince Charles appears to be experiencing. All of these royal mothers have broken the rules. Good mothers do not cavort half-naked with male friends in the presence of their children. Nor do good mothers spend Christmas, a crucial family time, apart from their children. Nor do good mothers spend endless time away from their children on foreign trips and then greet them frostily when they return. To behave in these ways is seen to be damaging to children and selfish on the part of the mother. It is seen to be the very antithesis of the natural behaviour of a good mother. Moreover, the public world makes it clear that they have behaved in an unnatural way by placing a very powerful sanction on them – public disapproval.

Being a stepmother is very closely related to being a mother. Your role is two-fold.

- firstly, to undertake the wide range of domestic duties that are associated with running a house and bringing up children;
- secondly, to be responsible for the way your children turn out.

In both of these areas, the stepmother's job can be extremely difficult. Being a mother and stepmother involves spending long hours with children and spending that time closeted in the home – longer, in fact, than fathers and stepfathers who stereotypically may be out at work or who may not see their role as having much to do with children.

The amount of direct contact you have with your step-children can therefore impact on how you experience your role. Indeed, research on motherhood generally indicates how isolating and debilitating it can be bringing up children. One very telling area of the effects of this is the number of women taking tranquillisers and anti-depressants. In Britain, as in most other Western countries, one in five women take tranquillisers. In the United States there are around 5 million women who are alcoholic. These figures clearly indicate that the cost of doing such a hard job is immense in terms of women suffering.

In addition, mothers are held by society to be answerable for the upbringing of children in their care. This can range from being seen to be responsible for how stepchildren are dressed to whether they stay out of trouble at school or with the police. These high expectations we have of mothers are similarly placed on stepmothers. Stepmothers have a lot of pressure and responsibility placed upon their shoulders.

Remember: What makes a good stepmother is the same as that which makes a good mother.

Temptress or Angel?

Whilst stepmothers have to contend with the nature of the expectations I've outlined, they also have to deal with assumptions about their cruel nature. The wicked step-mother myths are well outlined in almost all books on the stepfamily. Cinderella and Snow White suffered abysmally at the hands of cruel and unloving stepmothers who connived to get rid of them. These tales portray a woman's nature as devious and imbued with mysterious powers. They suggest she can be fearsome and should not be trusted. Indeed, much feminist scholarship has pointed out how women can be seen on the one hand to be the evil temptress and on the other hand the perfect mother. We only have to think of the images of Eve, Adam's temptress, and the Virgin Mary to under-stand this. Psychological theories similarly understand the contradiction between the mother and stepmother image in terms of splitting these two roles into good and evil. Such theories argue that children need to preserve an image of their natural mother as good. Therefore, the stepmother has to be bad. Tough on the stepmum!

As we know, these tales are still very much with us today to reinforce on our children the terrors that result from having a stepmother. Evidence of their strength as some-thing that creates a problem for women rather than men lies in the fact that whilst there is little evidence of stepmothers being abusers of children, there is a good number of cases of children being physically and sexually abused by their stepfathers. Yet stepfathers don't appear in the popular imagination as essentially wicked in the way that step-mothers do. So acting wickedly, it appears, is like child-birth. It is something only women can do!

These therefore constitute the conditions which contribute to making stepmotherhood one of the most difficult of family roles our society has to offer. It is a role that fits in-between all kinds of other roles. You're not quite a mother, but you're more than a friend. How do you cope? Our next step is to consider how these conditions affect the way you experience being a stepmother.

THE SUPERSTEPMOM

Are you a superstepmom, the kind of stepmother who feels she has to do absolutely everything for her family whatever the cost to herself? Many stepmothers fall into this trap. It is the price of the expectations and penalties placed on step-mothers that we have just discussed. If you are to be the angel not the witch you really have no alternative. Or do you?

Have you ever stopped to consider what you do and why? Both the quantity and the reason? Have you ever stopped to question how the structure of your life affects the way you feel about it? Overwork in itself can lead to tiredness and depression. Have you ever stopped to think how your role as a stepmother is defined by the society we live in? That is, how the expectations we have just briefly discussed affect the way we assess what is right and wrong?

We know that much is expected from a stepmother. She has to be all the things a mother is, but without the naturalness inherent in relationships between mothers and their children. A stepmother is simply a stand-in mother. Being a stand-in mother is a lot of physical hard work and a lot of social and family responsibility. And most of all it's wrapped up in the word 'caring'.

I want to spend some time on both these aspects of a stepmother's caring role: the physical labour involved in stepmothering and the responsibility.

My aim is to encourage you to consider how they impact

on your life and your relationships in your stepfamily. An understanding of these areas is central to being successful as a stepmother.

Remember: Caring is both labour and responsibility.

Caring as Labour

Doing the housework isn't the stuff normally associated with stepfamily problems. It is one of the taken-for-granted features of a woman's life. Why then should we be so concerned about it? Perhaps because it is so taken for granted. Because we unthinkingly do the cleaning, washing, shopping and cooking, we forget that housework *is* work. But as unpaid work, it somehow doesn't count. We don't hear of housewives clocking off at five o'clock, putting their feet up and having a gin and tonic, the day's work done. Rather we consider that going out into the alien world of paid work is more arduous and deserves such treatment. Whilst the husband's dinner may be on the table at the end of the day, who gets the houseworking wife's?

You can't even win if you do engage in paid work. Research is replete with examples of women now doing what is known as the dual shift. That is, they go out to their part- or full-time paid work and return to continue working on domestic chores in the home. Going out to work hasn't shifted the burden, it's doubled it. One stepmother I knew was fortunate enough to be able to afford paid help. She herself worked outside the home full-time. She commented to me how wonderful it was to come back to a cup of tea made and an unwinding chat. 'It's just like having a wife,' she said. We all need a wife. Unfortunately, it seems only men get one!

How much time do you spend caring for your stepfamily? Research has been conducted which indicates that mothers with children under one year old spend fourteen hours a day on average on childcare and housework. Men spend one hour a day. A bit of a disparity, isn't it? There is little to suggest that the ratio diminishes tremendously as children get older.

The household division of labour in stepfamilies is no different. Despite there being many different types of family these days, the belief in a division of labour in the house based on male and female roles is still very strong in our society. Statistics from a survey in 1988 called 'British Social Attitudes' indicated that 82% of women were mainly responsible for general domestic duties and care of children. As Hilary Graham says so pertinently in her book *Hardship and Health in Women's Lives*, even in the 1990s few women achieve an equal partnership when the household tasks are divided up.

Many women also appear to agree that such a division of labour is right and proper. It is their main function in life and part of their self-identity. Yet for the stepmother this can result in very contradictory feelings. On the one hand it's the right way to organise family life. On the other it creates a growing sense of injustice. Why should she do all this work for other people's children, especially as it usually receives little thanks? This is fertile ground for resentment to prosper. In addition, housework is physically tiring and leaves little time for other activities. In particular, it leaves little time for the stepmother to call her own. Here are the experiences of two stepmothers:

> 'What really upsets me is you spend all this time looking after other people and then at the end you haven't got time for yourself. I mean they treat you like a mother when they want something, like an invader when they've got everything and where's the thanks? I try to do my best, I really do. But sometimes it drives me batty.'

> 'I struggle with the housework like everyone does. They [stepchildren] don't help me. I wouldn't ask them. John [stepson] tidies his room. I vacuum it. If I didn't it would never get done. They don't do anything round here. It's like pushing uphill getting them to do the simplest thing. So I resent them. I can't win there. So that's not very easy.'

We can see, therefore, that the effect of being a superstepmom means that stepmothers:

- have little time they can call their own
- are frequently exhausted
- work extremely hard in all kinds of taken-for-granted ways
- can feel resentful at the load imposed on them.

ACTIVITY

Are you a superstepmom?

Make a list of everything you have done today. Include everything from dusting to phoning your mother, from ferrying step/children to and from their friends to helping with homework.

TODAY I HAVE:

This is an important activity. It will help you to:

- have some comprehension of the amount of work you do;
- look for areas of overload;
- start to prioritise things in your life.

Did you realise you did quite so much? It's quite shocking, isn't it, to see it written down? Now take stock. Ask yourself the following questions. Use them to reflect on areas where you could make changes.

- What do I see as the main reasons why I do all these activities?

- How do I feel about doing all these things?
- Are they all absolutely necessary?
- Are there any activities I particularly resent doing? Why?
- Are there any activities I particularly like doing? Why?
- Could any of these activities be shared within the family to lighten the load a little?
- Is it worth engaging/can I afford domestic help?
- What is the worst that would happen if I didn't do all this?

Remember: When you look back over your life, you won't wish you'd spent more time on housework. So why waste your life now?

KNOWING THE PRESSURE TIMES IN YOUR LIFE

For many stepmothers there are particular times of the day or week when they feel especially vulnerable to that sense of overload. For some stepmothers, whose stepchildren visit but do not live permanently with them, this can be weekends. For others, it can be a particular time in the day. One stepmother I know, with two young children and two teenage step-children, found that early evening was her most pressured point. This is what she wrote in a diary she kept for me:

5.00 p.m. Got tea for children. Very tired and irritable. I hate this time of day when there's a meal to get, clearing up to do and children to get bathed and to bed.

Days and weeks have patterns to them. Getting children off to school in the morning, cooking an evening meal, access visits are part of the regularity of stepfamily life. Visiting step-children at weekends add to the workload, with extra meals to cook and more clearing up to do. Get to know your pressured times.

ACTIVITY

When do the pressures occur?

- Keep a time diary for one week or even one month. Note down the times and days of the week when you are regularly involved in caring activities.
- Asterisk or star those times when you feel under pressure.
- Note down your feelings at these times.

TIME DIARY	DAY	
Time	Activity	Response

This is an important activity. It will help you to:

- know when your overload points are in your day/week/month;
- look at your patterns of response;
- begin to distinguish between relationship problems and overload.

Now take stock. Ask yourself the following questions:

- When are my most busy times?
- Is there any relationship between these times and when:
  - I feel I cannot cope with being a stepmother?
  - I get angry with my partner?
  - I get angry with my step/children?
  - I am more likely to be reduced to tears?

Keeping a time diary is a good way of finding the potential flashpoints in your life. It will help you to see the link between the patterns of your daily life and your up-and-down mood swings. It will help you to begin to distinguish between personality clashes between stepmother and step-children and those clashes which occur when life is simply getting too much. But knowing is only half the battle. Action is also required if you are going to change your life.

Use your time diary:

- as a point of discussion with your partner and, if possible, step/children. Show them how much you are doing. They will probably be surprised at the quantity when they see it recorded in this manner. Discuss ways of:
  - enlisting their support in doing some of the chores;
  - their being more sensitive to your needs at overload points;
  - if all else fails, knowing when to avoid you!
- to find some personal space. This is one of the most important things I can say and I cannot stress it enough. Women are the worst at rewarding or giving to them-selves, at taking some space. Take some time just for you. Have a bath on your own with the door locked. Sit in the living room in front of your favourite TV programme. Buy yourself that dress you like. Anything. But acknowledge that you have needs too.

Remember: If you don't value yourself, why should anyone else?

These activities have been designed to help you to assess how the sheer quantity of work you do in the house, as part of your caring activities, can contribute to a sense of dissatisfac-tion and unfairness in your life. Let us now consider the second aspect of caring which is part of the job of being a stepmother, that of responsibility.

CARING AS RESPONSIBILITY

Are you a supermom? If the outcome of the exercises you have just completed indicates that you spend the majority of your time running round after children, doing everything for them, or almost everything, then you are a supermom. But being a supermom is something more than physically doing a lot of work. These are the more outward signs of a mental attitude towards how you see your role in life. Feelings of responsibility also go with the territory of being a stepmother. They add another dimension to your life which can quickly turn into a feeling that you carry the responsibility alone. One stepmother I know has experienced many difficulties in recent years with her teenage stepson. From time to time these reach crisis point. Bitter arguments result in her husband saying that his son, her stepson, must go. He cannot stand the atmosphere and disruption he sees his son causing in their family life. What she finds remarkable is that at this point she intercedes. She is the one who says she cannot allow this to happen. The boy must not leave. She says this, despite the fact that she too can only see the end of this animosity through him leaving home. Why does she stop him? Because if he leaves, she sees that she has failed in her responsibility to him. As a stepmother she takes that responsibility far more seriously than the father.

Another stepmother I know also took her responsibilities very seriously. She considered that she should be the person who should work at maintaining good relationships with her stepchildren's mother. The mother was the non-custodial parent and the children lived full-time with their father and stepmother. The stepmother thought a good relationship with the mother was important for the children's sake and so would invite the mother into her house, have chats with her over cups of tea and encourage as much access as possible. However, she told me that her husband did not like her to have such a good relationship with his ex-wife. From his point of view, the less the children saw of their mother the better. He wanted her out of their lives altogether. So, although the stepmother was taking very seriously her responsibilities, this was being undermined by the father.

Responsibility is, in fact, another of those taken-for-granted aspects of family life that we rarely stop to think about. Women expect to take responsibility for the welfare of their family. Stepmothers are only carrying on the tradition. Indeed, the behaviour of the stepmothers above shows us the strengths that stepmothers can bring to the stepfamily. They can step back and put the needs of the child first. However, responsibility can also, at times, be a heavy weight to bear. In particular, if you fail in your responsibility, you can experience strong feelings of guilt and responsibility itself can create a feeling of overload.

Let us work through some of this by firstly taking a look at the areas of responsibility that you take on board. This will give you an opportunity to stop working on automatic pilot and question some of the assumptions we make about our lives.

ACTIVITY

Assess the ways in which you feel responsible.
Complete the following:

The responsibilities of mothers are:
Hygiene/feeding/managing   housekeeping/cleaning/ clothing children/discipline/health of family/education of children/shopping.
(*Add or delete as appropriate*)

The responsibilities of fathers are:
Family's financial income/organising holidays/gardening/car/discipline/decorating/house maintenance . . .
(*Add or delete as appropriate*)

The responsibilities of stepmothers are:
(*Put your personal list here*)

This is an important activity. It will help you to:

● see clearly your responsibilities as a stepmother;
● see clearly the responsibilities which are not a step-mother's;
● see clearly areas of overlap.

Now take stock. Look at your answers to the activity above and ask the following questions to reflect on how responsibility shapes your life and your attitudes.

● What do I see myself as responsible for?
● Why have I given these responses to the questions?
● What does the pattern of responses suggest about my attitudes and views?
● Do I see these areas of responsibility related to the appropriate roles for men and women or natural parents and stepparents.

You should now be in a position where you have some understanding of how you have divided responsibilities in your life between your family members. You will also have an understanding of those areas which you feel particularly strongly are mainly your responsibility. You will also know where there is overlap or ambiguity. This is an important insight, particularly as this is an area which causes untold animosity between stepparents and non-custodial parents. Specifically, stepmothers are often left in a situation where they feel they, or their husbands, are carrying all the responsibilities for meeting children's needs. It appears to them that the natural mother contributes nothing in this respect. One stepmother I know felt that she and her husband were left to foot all the costs of their children visiting their maternal grandparents and mother. This was her experience:

'Every year my stepchildren's grandparents would invite them over for a holiday in Spain where they had retired. Of course the children wanted to go. What would get my goat, though, was their mother would also be there having a holiday with them. She never offered to pay for their fare though. Nothing. In fact she was such a sponger she even got her parents to pay for her.

'We couldn't ask the grandparents. That didn't seem fair. But she [the mother] could have paid something. After all, it was her parents they were visiting. We were the ones making sure that the children didn't lose touch with their grandparents. We could easily have said no. It would have been much cheaper. But you can't do that. It's not right. So we'd spend two days taking them to the airport and back. And having to find the air fare. The children thought it was great. Especially as they saw it that it was a holiday with Mum. As if she'd contributed something.'

We can see that the issue of responsibility can be an area fraught with hazards in maintaining good relationships with children's natural parents. One of the reasons why step-mothers continue to carry out these responsibilities is because of the penalties attached if you don't. What happens, for example, if you do feel you are being neglectful of your right and proper duties? Feeling neglectful is danger-ous. It leads to guilt and a concern that the world will think you don't really care about your stepchildren. This was a very common occurrence in my own research. One stepmother, in full-time work, became very worried that she couldn't attend her stepdaughter's school open day. 'How will she feel if I don't go?' was her concern. 'What will the teachers think?' If she didn't go she would not be fulfilling her duties as a responsible and caring stepmother. Interestingly, her response is comparable to the stepmother we have just mentioned who could not allow her stepson to be banished from the family home. She feels responsibility, whereas the child's natural father was unconcerned. In fact he told his wife not to worry and added, 'I'm often too busy to go to these school things.' Why then should she feel so responsible? After all, her husband – the child's natural parent – wasn't worried. And the child's natural mother, who happened to live just two miles down the road, was also apparently unconcerned. This is another instance where there is a duplication of responsibility. Should the stepmother feel that it is up to her to attend parents' evenings when the biological parents do not? Is there something so in-bred in stepmothers that if we don't meet society's high standards we have failed. And in failure there is guilt.

When things go wrong with children or with families, as Donna Smith says, the mother is blamed. For stepmothers, the situation is even worse and the stepmother can be a scapegoat. One of the reasons for this is because the stepmother is a living embodiment of the end of the first natural family. When things go wrong, therefore, all the negative feelings we have about failed marriage and stepfamilies generally fall on the stepmother who is seen to be responsible for the children in her charge. The stepmother has failed in her duties in just the same way as the Queen, Princess Diana and Fergie have been seen to do. Their children's failures, or likely failures in the future, are the result of bad mothering. The stepchild's failures are seen to be the result of bad stepmothering.

What is the answer to this dilemma? How can we fulfil all the expectations placed on us and which we put upon ourselves? The answer is very hard, you can't. Not without running round like a headless chicken, trying to be all things to everybody but with no direction, and running yourself into the ground at the same time. 'Ah,' you say, 'that's all very well for you to say, but if I don't do all these things I risk being socially ostracised and bringing on myself a massive amount of guilt.' Well, I never said life would be easy!

ACTIVITY

Getting your responsibilities into perspective.

1 Order your responsibilities.
Look at your list of stepmother responsibilities. Put them in order of how pressurised they make you feel. Score them out of 100. The most pressurised will be closer to 100. The least pressurised will be closer to 0.

2 Divide your score by 3. Now you need to reduce your responsibilities by the resulting number. That is by one-third. You can do this by:
- delegating whole tasks to other family members who may also be responsible for them. Look back at those that overlap, for example.
- sharing certain responsibilities with your partner. This will reduce their score by half. Log this as something you need to talk to him about.
- deleting any tasks which are superfluous.

This is an important activity. It will help you to:

- consider how you can change some aspects of your responsibilities without causing untold damage to your family;
- accept you are human – let yourself off the hook sometimes.

Remember: The first rule of management is delegation. So manage those responsibilities now and delegate, delegate, delegate.

We have so far explored the ways in which stepmothers are expected to behave as much as possible like any mother in the land. We have considered how this can cause stresses and strains in stepmothers' lives, as indeed they do in mothers' lives. We now reach the next step in achieving success as a stepmother. We need to look at some of the unique experiences of being a stepmother.

THE DISTINCTIVE EXPERIENCES OF STEPMOTHERHOOD

How on earth do you deal with a world that is intent on perceiving you as rather nasty? Stepmothers throughout the world face this dilemma. This idea of wickedness has a rather malicious habit of seeping into all parts of your life affecting the things you can and can't do. We consider how the stepmother myth affects your life by looking at three areas: self-esteem, anger and discipline.

We start off by asking, how did we get to be wicked stepmothers in the first place?

FROM FAIRY GODMOTHER TO WICKED STEPMOTHER

> **Love seeketh not itself to please,**
> **Nor for itself hath any care,**
> **But for another gives its ease,**
> **And builds a Heaven in Hell's despair.**
> **(William Blake, 1757–1827)**

Was this the picture you had in mind when you fell in love? To build a heaven in hell's despair? This is indeed the picture most stepmothers have in their minds when they are beginning to think of becoming part of a stepfamily. The hell is the life the father and children have experienced since the break-up of the family. The heaven is the happy family you are going to create. In fact at this early point in the relationship, you haven't become the wicked stepmother yet. You are in fact the Fairy Godmother appearing as some latter-day saviour. Listen to these stepmothers talk about their thoughts on life in a stepfamily at the beginning of the relationship:

'I had this picture in my head of travelling in the car on holiday with these two children in the back. His. Everything was sunny and happy. I thought they'd been through a terrible time with the loss of their mother. Jim and I getting together would mean that we would be a normal family. Doing happy things together.'

'I knew Nic had children when we met. I didn't think it would matter. In fact, I thought it'd be quite nice having them come over, you know, at weekends. We could be a family together. With me as this warm mother figure.'

'I was going to rewrite the book on wicked stepmothers. I was going to be the best stepmother there was.'

What appears to happen is that the stepmother sees herself as a Fairy Godmother who is going to make up for the bad times of the past. Helen Franks, in *Remarriage*, uses the work of a Gestalt therapist Patricia Papernow to describe this phase as Fantasy. She says this is the first stage of 'romantic rescue ... when a prospective stepparent has high hopes of an instant cure for the family's past unhappiness'.

Why, we need to consider, should this be the case? Partly, I think, because being without a partner in our society makes one an Odd Woman. George Gissing's novel of the same name is a good source of insight here. His novel takes place in the 19th century and shows clearly the vicissitudes of being single. In the late 20th century it certainly appears that all the world's a couple, except you. This makes for loneliness and a feeling of being an outsider. Add to this trying to get over a broken marriage, reorder your life, look after children as a lone parent and it is no wonder you yearn for that sense of security as a couple. One of the stepmothers in my own research study described how her first husband died very suddenly in his mid-20s. She gave birth to her second child a few days later. Her sorrow and grief at her husband's death was tinged with happiness at the birth of her daughter. Such a mixture of emotion. As the months passed, however, she felt indescribable loneliness and hardship trying to bring up two young children alone. She said, 'You live and eat pain.' Eventually she met, and quickly married, her second husband. She had recoupled and recreated a 'normal' family.

Another reason why we may be so willing to enter the fantasy stage is that little thought is given to the implications of our actions. Research indicates that the majority of adults, male or female, who become stepparents actually give little thought to the realities of what they are doing. Love is a powerful emotion. Many stepmothers have told me how they 'viewed things through rose-coloured spectacles' or 'didn't think there were too many difficulties' or 'didn't really think about it', mainly because they considered that the love they felt for their new partner would be sufficient to overcome all obstacles.

Unfortunately, as Helen Franks neatly puts it, 'then comes a rude awakening'. It is at this point that the Fairy Godmother gives way to the Wicked Stepmother in the stepmother's perception of herself.

Enter the Wicked Stepmother: Exit Self-esteem

This rude awakening can of course take many forms: a realisation that there are aspects of your stepchildren's behaviour you don't like and even find intolerable; a feeling of being let down by your new partner who appears to prefer to keep his children and ex happy rather than you; the intrusion of access visits. In addition, financial worries, continuing legal problems, living in someone else's house, turn a potentially fulfilling relationship into pure burden. Through an ongoing series of continual arguments, stormy scenes and icy silence, together with feelings of anger and hatred, you begin to see yourself acting out the Wicked Stepmother myth. Yes, you would like these children to get lost in a forest and never return. How can you help them on their way?

This is what one stepmother had to say:

'Before I became a stepmother I used to think I was quite a nice person. Becoming a stepmother led me to discover parts of my character I would have chosen not to know! I act, and am, at times, the real wicked stepmother. I can hate, loathe and detest. I can wish nasty things would happen to certain people who entered my life. I can shout, scream and bitch. I couldn't believe the harridan I could become at the slightest provocation – access visits, his ex-wife on the doorstep or even her phoning. Well, the whole of stepfamily life in fact.'

The effect of this on your self-esteem is to demoralise you totally. Tears are frequent and it is hard to dislodge a self-image of your new-found witch-like character. You begin to feel you are going slightly insane. If that's not enough, you also begin to feel that others around you see you as neurotic. How many times have you been told that you are mad or barmy? Research indicates that women in general go through life with very low self-esteem. Part of the reason for this is that we are taught from childhood that we don't count. The experience of being told you don't count throughout your life soon makes you believe it. Women therefore take second place in the order of things and come to see this as natural and appropriate.

Unfortunately, low self-esteem can affect every aspect of your life. You feel you are incapable of taking on responsibility at work, have a negative body image and can be depressed. Low self-esteem is seen to be contributory to over-eating problems and alcoholism. It is pernicious because it is so common. We are used to feeling this way. When we meet women who have self-respect and high esteem we denigrate them. We think they are over-confident and bossy. Yet low self-esteem can in fact mean that we don't reach our full potential as human beings. We see ourselves as under-achievers and so become under-achievers. There is enough in stepfamily life to reinforce these attitudes – all the slights and hurts. Do me a favour though. Challenge those negative thoughts now.

ACTIVITY

Build your self-esteem. Knowing the put-downs.

---

1   Begin by thinking of any put-downs you may have experienced as a child. Were you told you were stupid, silly, lazy, naughty, even wicked? Can you think how this might affect how you see yourself today?

2   Think now about your current situation. Do people tell you that you worry too much, or go over the top or make a fuss about nothing. If so, do these comments tell you your understandings must be wrong? If you have been told you're wrong in some way, as a child, how do these adult put-downs reinforce your image of yourself?

This is an important activity. It will help you:

- understand how your self-esteem can stem from the way you are treated;
- become conscious of put-downs;
- challenge the put-downs. How true are they?

This exercise will help you to see that your image of yourself can be moulded by other people. Realising this can help you to see that the slightest comment, innocent or not, can affect the way you think about yourself. Now work on developing a positive attitude about yourself.

ACTIVITY

Build your self-esteem. Learn to love yourself.

---

1 List your achievements, whatever they are. Can you drive a car? Are you good at flower arranging? Do you sew or knit? Do you work full-time and still manage to run a home? Don't denigrate even the smallest accomplishment. They are positive building blocks.

2 Savour compliments. Women are terrible at rejecting compliments. Don't. Take them for what they are – someone telling you how wonderful you are.

3 Think of the things about yourself that you like. Can you think of one thing, maybe two, even three? It's hard because we are so used to putting ourselves down. But it's worthwhile. Try it every day. Learn not to underestimate yourself.

This is an important activity. It will help you:

- build your self-confidence;
- appreciate that you do have much to offer your stepfamily.

Remember: You are the greatest. You are a stepmother.

Low self-esteem can also be reinforced by expressions of anger. Anger can be such a demoralising emotion. Let our next step be to consider how we can cope with this.

ANGER

Expressing anger is one of the areas where women feel least comfortable. When we get angry it goes against everything that we have been taught we should be – kind, loving, gentle, caring and passive. Anger is an active emotion, even if we express it passively by bottling it up. Being angry can mean that we are not behaving in ways that are acceptable for women to behave. There is, therefore, a double jeopardy in feeling anger. It leaves us with a sense of failure, inadequacy, depression and vulnerability. It leaves us with a sense that we are not very feminine. These feelings can leave us totally annihilated, even to the extent that we feel we must ourselves leave home, as this mother expresses so well:

'Before Christmas, Pam [stepdaughter] and I had a massive argument. By the end of the night I felt so wretched. It left me in a state. I said I'd have to move out. I felt physically sick. I was in a complete state, really the works.'

For stepmothers, anger can also reinforce their fear that the world will see them as wicked. The good, kindly, even-tempered mother is the public and personal image we want to create about ourselves. Expressions of anger can dent that image. There is in fact a lovely quote from Cherie Burns in her book, *Stepmotherhood*, about the extent to which stepmothers will go to avoid being viewed as wicked. She says, 'Most stepmothers will verge on the masochistic in order to assure themselves and anyone who's watching that they are not wicked.' How right she is. Stepmothers not only behave as the superstepmom but the fear of being a real wicked step-mother feeds into almost every area of a stepmother's life, even if this means the suppression of their feelings and needs. To be angry does nothing for your self-esteem, fragile as it is. But I have to tell you, in some circumstances it is perfectly natural to get and feel angry. It is also very common.

One way of helping yourself to deal with anger is to learn to overcome your conditioning that anger isn't acceptable. The seeming unacceptability of anger can have a very debilitating effect on your morale as a stepmother. It can feed into your heartfelt fears that you are indeed wicked. In addition, stepmothers cannot guarantee that their expres-sions of anger will remain private. Stepchildren, who travel between two homes, are seen to be carriers of messages that tell the rival mother that you really are cranky. As one stepmother put it, 'If I've had a benny [argument] I'd always regret it afterwards. I could almost feel their mother laughing at me as if she knew.'

One of the features of being a stepmother is that you feel that you are the only one who feels and acts this way. Why? Because it is relatively rare that we see other stepmothers' expressions of anger. This is what I would see as the conspiracy of stepmotherhood. We hide behind veils of moderate, even-handed behaviour in our public displays of ourselves. Yet, as a researcher, I feel I was very privileged to have insight into how common anger was as an expression of feeling for stepmothers. It helped me to see my own behaviour as less abnormal and more the result of my situation. One stepmother, I remember, told me how she had had an argument with her husband and had thrown something through the bedroom window, breaking the glass. Hearing this, I no longer felt so bad about myself, knowing that I too was prone to throwing and breaking things! Whilst I hasten to add I'm not advocating we go around wrecking our homes to get rid of pent-up frustration, knowing that others act and feel the same means you can at least stop berating yourself for your behaviour. I hope that knowledge helps you too.

In addition, you may find it useful to consider ways that you can make anger work positively for you. Anger doesn't come as a visitation from the gods. It has a cause. If you can find the cause you are on your way to dealing with your anger appropriately.

ACTIVITY

What makes you angry?

1 Look back at the exercises you have already done. They will help you to identify those times when you have become angry. They will also have highlighted stress and fatigue points – those times when you would have to be a saint not to get a bit hot under the collar. Are there any changes in your life you could make to help you manage these occasions in a way that doesn't lead to overload?

2 Ask yourself who you get angry with. Do you get angry more often with particular people, say a step-child? Would spending less time with this person help? Do you take your anger out on a particular person who isn't really the cause of your distress? If so, explaining that they are the whipping post may help your relationship.

3 Ask yourself why you feel angry. Do you have a long-standing grievance that continues unresolved? Can you make any changes that will settle the situation?

4 Ask yourself how you feel when you get angry? Having a good shouting match might relieve the tension. It might also make you feel demoralised and ashamed. Know how you feel so that you don't constantly put yourself in situations that make you feel bad after the event.

This is an important activity. It will help you:

- identify some of the causes of your anger;
- identify some of the solutions to those causes.

Remember: You are allowed to get angry. Sometimes it's only natural.

DISCIPLINE: THE STEPMOTHER'S DILEMMA

Help! How do I discipline my stepchildren and still not turn them against me? One of the most important, and potentially problematic, areas of the need not to be seen as wicked is that of disciplining stepchildren. Here the masochistic stepmother avoids the act of discipline with fervour and ingenuity. Why? Because discipline is essentially a negative act. It has the potential of making you appear and act in rather unattractive ways. We've all seen the mother in the supermarket shouting at her children for picking up sweets or running round. She may be right, but it's not very nice to witness, is it? The act of discipline can also make you feel bad in yourself. None of us really likes being punitive – it doesn't make us feel good about ourselves. So the stepmother sees herself as not only acting in a wicked way but she feels wicked into the bargain.

My experience of stepmotherhood suggests that as far as discipline is concerned, stepmothers use the following tactics:

- avoiding confrontation
- ignoring the situation
- getting your partner to do it

Let us look at how each one works.

Avoiding confrontation

Staying silent about things that annoy you is one strategy that stepmothers employ to avoid being seen as wicked. In this way, you can maintain an outward appearance that all is OK whilst inside you're seething. An example of this happened to me whilst I was interviewing stepmothers for my own research study. One stepmother, Susan, had a three-year-old daughter and when I came to talk to her one day she asked her older stepdaughter to look after the little girl so that we could talk without interruption. Midway through our chat, the stepdaughter came in and said she was going out. Susan made no attempt to ask her if she could wait a little longer until we had finished. She simply said, 'OK.' Her step-daughter left and her three-year-old joined us. It was at this point that Susan expressed her exasperation at her step-daughter's behaviour. It meant our conversation had to stop but she felt powerless to do anything about it.

This feeling of powerlessness also applies to other step-child behaviour, for example, wanting help around the house. The supermom stepmother simply feels she cannot ask for it. Rather than treating her stepchildren as potential Cinderellas or Cinderfellas, stepmothers avoid the confronta-tion. Elizabeth Hodder comments on this in terms of the 'stepmother as nag'. She quite rightly points out that it is very difficult as a stepmother to nag without seeming to be an ogress. This is because you are not part of the fixtures and fittings in a way that a natural mother is. Therefore it is easy to feel that your 'nagging' will be seen as an aspect of your witch-like behaviour. Much better to avoid confrontation, or even ignore the situation.

Ignoring the situation

Ignoring the need to discipline is one common way of avoiding the label 'wicked'. This type of strategy might rely on the hope that if you don't take any notice, the behaviour will miraculously disappear. But it can be rooted in a fear that you lack the authority, as a stepmother, to challenge chil-dren's behaviour. You are not, after all, their proper parent. Let me give you an example of this kind of behaviour from my own research:

> **Jane, Simon and the children had all gone out to a restaurant for a meal. Angela, Jane's stepdaughter, aged 8, did not eat her dinner. She said she felt unwell. Jane kept silent. Pudding was ordered. Angela made a miraculous recovery and wanted some ice cream. Jane murmured to Simon that in her opinion**

she shouldn't have any since she had left her dinner. Simon murmured his agreement to Jane and promptly let Angela have her ice cream!

Note the role reversal in this situation. Jane does not carry any natural authority to control Angela's eating behaviour. If Jane had been her natural mother she would have been able to and probably would have done so quite automatically. Telling your children they can't have pudding until they've eaten their dinner is pretty common. In this situation, Jane kept quiet. She deemed it inappropriate to say anything. Jane is left frustrated at what she sees is wrongful behaviour.

Note however how Jane has whispered to Simon her feelings on the subject of Angela's behaviour. This is a clear signal for him to intervene. This is the final strategy I want us to consider.

Getting your partner to do it

Don't want to shout at the stepchildren? Want to chastise them for their terrible behaviour? Then get your partner to do the disciplining for you. After all, they're his children, not yours! The benefit of this strategy is that it clearly avoids placing yourself in an invidious position. You can take a back seat but still try to evoke some change. This is, in fact, a very common stepmother strategy when it comes to discipline or any other behaviour that she wishes to change in her stepchildren.

A stepmother may ask her partner to intervene when she does not feel she has the authority of a parent, or when any attempt by her to ask her stepchildren to close the door, tidy their room, stop using the phone so much, is met by antagonism and resentment. Here the stepmother feels that the stepchild is focusing all their resentment on her as the cause of all the child's trouble. This was one stepmother's experience of the impossibility of her situation, in which there is a clear correlation between discipline and the stepmother herself being seen to be the wicked one:

'I tend to be doing that more now [asking her partner to intervene] because I'm getting an attitude "I won't be told by you." Harry has to be the one to tell her [stepdaughter]. Suddenly I was getting "What a horrible stepmother you are." Anything I said just made it worse. He has to tell her things.'

The problems of these strategies

These approaches to discipline may indeed be an appropriate strategy in the early stages of your relationship when you clearly lack a persona as an authority figure. In the early days your main concerns are to build a positive and happy relationship with stepchildren, not to appear the ogre or disciplinarian. Indeed, whilst you may be planning to be around for a good while, from the child's perspective you're a relative stranger. Getting heavy is therefore unlikely to ingratiate you with them.

While this is fine in the short term, there are problems associated with each of these strategies:

- avoiding confrontation leaves you seething;
- ignoring the situation doesn't change anything;
- using your partner doesn't always work and in the end makes him angry with you.

Let's look at these problems in more detail. It is clear from the above examples that both avoiding confrontation and ignoring the situation are very much short-term or intermittent tactics. They are certainly useful in that 'getting to know the stepchildren' stage and should never be ditched for this very reason. In addition, they are extremely useful for taking the heat out of a situation that is reaching boiling point. Walking away from confrontation can defuse potential problems which might otherwise get out of hand. However, avoiding confrontation and ignoring the situation are not solutions that can be used for every occasion. They leave you feeling you have no control whatsoever over your situation.

Getting your partner to do the disciplining is also not

terribly effective. Experience suggests that you will not be satisfied at the way your partner, as your proxy, disciplines the children. Principally, from your point of view, he will probably be too lenient, leaving you boiling with frustration that he has not sorted the problem out. Indeed, in the longer run, the problem won't be sorted out. As one stepmother put it:

'Very often when I want Pete to say something he doesn't say the complete thing. He'll tiptoe round things. Then I feel like I heard that. That was a waste of time. Nothing changes. In the end I still have to say because it doesn't get done.'

Secondly, using your partner as a go-between in the end will alienate him. What you are doing is placing him in a punitive role when all he wants to do is make up for all the hard times the children have been through. He probably feels guilty enough without the burden of having to be the family ogre. In addition, you are putting him in the impossible situation of having to choose between you and his children. This is how one father experienced this:

'Often I felt piggy in the middle. My wife and my son would argue over something really stupid. She would lose her temper and he would shout back. She asked me to intervene but I couldn't. I really thought she was being unreasonable and that the situation had got out of hand. It had become a war and I became the mediator and was also expected to take sides. In the end my son would storm off, my wife wouldn't talk to me. Eventually I would get really wound up and go to see my son to sort it out. Support my wife as such. I'd find him reading a comic, laughing as if nothing had really happened. The only person it had cocked up was me and I didn't do anything.'

Another father confirms this experience in the following terms:

> **'The argument started without me here, carried on
> without my involvement. I pitched in at the end and
> the result was my wife told me she was going to leave
> me which meant I lost.'**

The situation of divided loyalties was expressed by one father
I know, whose partner is just ten years older than her
stepdaughter, as 'It's like two women arguing like sisters,
expecting me to be on both sides.' Indeed, as stepmothers we
know only too well that we are asking for our partner's
loyalty. As one stepmother aptly said, 'I see it as "it's them
or me". To me it's a pecking order situation.'

You need therefore to be able to discipline children
yourself but without becoming the family witch or turning
your partner against you.

ACTIVITY

How do you deal with discipline problems?

Think of a number of occasions when you have considered your stepchildren needed some kind of
reproach or sanction. Now answer the following questions about these occasions.
- How did you deal with these situations?
- Were your actions effective?
- Were you satisfied with the outcome each time?

This activity is important. It will help you to:

- consider your own strategies for discipline;
- think through the positive aspects of your approach;
- think through the negative aspects of your approach.

Use the knowledge you have gained about yourself from this
activity to think about whether the following ways of coping
with discipline problems would be appropriate for you.

GETTING HEARD WITHOUT SHOUTING: THE STEPMOTHER'S GUIDE

There are four main ways that are discussed here which may help you to establish and maintain your position as someone who is respected and who is listened to in your stepfamily. These are:

- building up your authority;
- getting support;
- taking the personal out of discipline;
- being opportune.

Build up your authority

As I've said, it takes time to build relationships within which there is some mutuality and respect. It is only after you have done this that your views and feelings will be listened to. Until you have had time to do this, there is really no harm in being lax with children. This may even get them on your side. Listen to this stepmother's strategy:

'I remember when I first began to live with my stepfamily, my stepson, then aged four, at breakfast was deliberately dropping cereal on the carpet. At the same time he was looking at me for my reaction. I was very tempted to shout at him for what he was doing. Making a right mess. But thankfully I didn't. Something stopped me. I decided to pretend it was sort of a game. But I knew he was testing me. So I winked and smiled at him. You know in a "I can see what you're up to" kind of way. He grinned back at me. Sort of impish like. We became a bit more like friends then.'

This stepmother's experience suggests that because she could be a little more relaxed about bad behaviour she was able to build up a relationship with her stepson. It is from this position that you can establish yourself as an authority figure.

Remember: It takes time to build relationships. Relax a little while you do.

Get support

One of the worst things about being in a stepfamily is that feeling of being an outsider, being alone. You are the inter-loper in the family. This feeling is not unique to stepmothers. But in this instance, there is nothing worse than feeling either that no one respects you or your views, or that you daren't express them for fear of being seen to be malevolent. Instead of placing your partner in an impossible position by asking him to do the work of disciplinarian, communicate with him. Try to decide some common grounds, especially if you are merging families with very different attitudes to discipline. But a word of warning about communication: as Deborah Fowler in her book *Loving Other People's Children* says, you should approach communication in the same way as sex therapists approach improving your sex life. Go slowly at first. Research shows that heart-to-hearts between partners are a normal element in the early stages of courtship of previously married couples. They have a therapeutic effect of working through the past. However, some of the issues you may wish to raise about your feelings towards step-children can be very threatening to your new partner. We may logically know that our children are no angels but hearing someone else tell you can be difficult to take. So go slowly. Be sensitive. But try.

Take the personal out of discipline

Can you remember thinking your parents were always having a go at you? The problem with discipline, from the child's point of view, is that this is exactly how she or he views it. You are having a go, for no good reason. When this happens you can be on a downward spiral. Each time you tell the child off it will be logged as yet another time that you've got a downer on him or her. So you need to take this personal element out of discipline. This can be especially important in a stepfamily where stepchildren consider favouritism is taking place. There is always the danger that, in their opinion, you let your own children, their stepbrothers and sisters, do as they please, but you're the real wicked stepmother with them. How do you take this personal element out of discipline? There are two ways:

- creating family rules;
- naming your mood.

Creating family rules

Creating a list of family rules can be a good starting point for giving yourself some legitimate authority. Recourse to the rules suggests forethought rather than reactive malevolence. It suggests fairness for all rather than favouritism and scapegoating. Such a list can be drawn up as a family enterprise which will enhance the likelihood that all members will take responsibility for it. Drawing up house rules should also be done with explanation. One stepmother, who was very worried about the costs of bringing up a large family – as stepfamilies inevitably are – decided some rules were necessary about the quantity and timing of baths. This would take advantage of cheaper off-peak electricity charges but would require some changes to the current practice of anyone taking a bath at any time. A list of times and bath rotas was set up to minimise cost and it was this element which was explained to all the children.

The list may not only include those items that reflect parental concerns. It can also be a time for children to express theirs. Drawing up a list of house rules can be a time to say that 'Jenny will not borrow Claire's clothes without asking' or 'Ben will not play with John's CD collection'.

Naming your mood

Despite the best of intentions, this more detached and potentially harmonious approach of rule-making will not work for every occasion. In particular, there is a range of problem areas which do not lend themselves easily to rule-making. They are what Deborah Fowler aptly calls the 'family wreckers', the little things which, as she says, can cause the biggest problems. As she points out the larger-than-life dramas of illness, financial ruin or even death do not split families. Indeed, they can bring families together. Rather, it is the little things, such as leaving doors open, lights on, muddy shoes on your carpet and dirty washing which really cause the problems. They get on your nerves in a pernicious way. They niggle at you until you explode. Indeed, this is the time when you are in danger of losing your temper and really acting out your wicked stepmother fears.

One way to act when things are really getting on top of you is to give your mood a name. One stepmother I knew was very good at this. When she was feeling low, or when things were getting on top of her, she would simply say to all her children – step and natural – 'Watch out, I'm on my broom-stick.' In other words, she gave a very clear signal to the children that her behaviour that day was not malicious, hurtful or personal. It was a signal to say she was in a bad mood, for good reason, and they had better watch out.

Be opportune

Attacking your stepson whilst he's in the middle of eating his dinner for the money he borrowed off you six months ago is not likely to encourage a positive response. Nor is asking for the replacement tights your stepdaughter promised when she last borrowed yours, if you time it just as her friends arrive. However, a pertinent comment or question at an appropriate moment is more likely to produce the response you want. This stepmother's comments show that she had tried the strategy of asking her husband to intervene, but that this did not work. In the end, she chose her moment wisely and solved her problem. This is what this stepmother told me:

'Anna [stepdaughter] had borrowed some money from her father for a deposit on a flat. She had some money

problems so she came back here to live. She came on the basis that she would pay us back when she could and would pay something towards her keep. This was five months ago. In that time she hasn't paid a penny back. But she can find money for other things. Anyway I told her father it was about time she paid some of it back and said he should ask her. Well, nothing happened. No money was forthcoming. Then one morning she had a bank statement and it was too good an opportunity. I told her she'd been here since August and that it added up to rather a lot of money. She didn't like it. I know she didn't. But she gave me a cheque.'

Money, it seems, is a particularly common area of concern and again one where stepmothers tread carefully or try to get their partners to act appropriately. As this stepmother says, money can be a sensitive issue and consequently needs to be dealt with carefully:

'I knew my stepdaughter had been borrowing money from her brother. My concern was that he wouldn't get it back. She also owed us money. She'd borrowed money from her Dad and was behind with her keep. It's uncomfortable for me to ask her. It's usually something her Dad does. Sometimes it'd be two or three weeks that she would owe us for keep. And then we'd hear that she was hard up. So it's harder to ask for it. Normally Eric [partner] asks for the money as it's a difficult subject anyway. But I knew at the moment she's loaded. She's just come back from working away and earned a lot of money. I told her how much she owed us. At first she was a bit funny about it. Said she didn't know if she could get that much out at once. If her pay cheque had cleared. But we got it.'

Choosing the right moment can therefore be a way of tackling difficult issues. By taking the matter successfully into your own hands it can also contribute to your sense of being in control of your life. You no longer have to wait for someone else, that is your partner, to act on your behalf.

These tactics are offered to you in the hope that they will enable you to manage one of the most difficult stepmother problems, being loved whilst maintaining some order and sanity in your life! Each will be useful for different problems, different occasions. Try them out. You might be surprised at the changes in your life.

REVIEW

The key messages of this chapter are:

- stepmothers do indeed have the hardest job;
- understand your problems by understanding your situation;
- stepmothers often try to be supermoms;
- the wicked stepmother myth is dangerous to self-esteem;
- discipline is difficult but these difficulties can be overcome. Just get on that broomstick and fly!

Remember: You are the superheroine. Who else would do what a stepmother does?

3

SUPERHEROES

'A stepfather is often a confused and worried man.' This quote from Elizabeth Hodder's book, *The Stepparents' Handbook*, may very well express just how you often feel. Trying to cope with the demands made of you by an ex-wife, a new wife, by children and stepchildren, not to mention the financial worries of paying maintenance and functioning effectively at work. However, in comparison to stepmothers, being a stepfather is not considered to be so onerous an experience. That is, it is not considered so onerous by researchers and commentators who have investigated the stepfather's role.

Why might this be the case? Mainly because the degree of difficulty that stepparents supposedly experience is linked to the extent of their contact with their stepchildren. It is thought therefore that as stepfathers, like fathers, traditionally have less direct contact with children, this reduced amount of physical proximity correspondingly reduces the problems experienced. Because you are out at work for long hours or because your normal responsibilities in the house do not include extensive care of children you are therefore thought to find the stepfather role less of a hassle.

I wonder how many stepfathers would actually agree that their role is not as difficult as the stepmother's. I know, from many stepfathers I have spoken to, that they do think that their partners sometimes make a mountain out of a molehill! However, whilst stepmothers may find the care of stepchildren at times particularly stressful, this is not saying that the stepfather's job is that easy. As I'm sure many of you will testify, it is not. Stepfathers in fact can face their own distinct problems which make the stepparenting task difficult and complex.

In this chapter we confront some of those difficulties by looking at the following issues:

- the pressures on men to be more responsive to their partner's and children's needs;
- the conflicts in being a father and a non-custodial parent;
- the stepfather as provider and disciplinarian;
- why men find themselves in the middle of stepfamily conflicts.

One of the ways in which we can see the difficulties which stepfathers experience is by recognising that the job of being a stepfather should not only be considered in relation to parenting other people's children. It should take a wider view. In addition to becoming a stepfather, such men are often a non-custodial parent of their own children. This can place them in an invidious position. They spend time with and influence their stepchildren in a way that they no longer do with their own. When seen in this light, we must agree that we ask a lot of such men.

Indeed, this situation can be exacerbated when we consider that men traditionally also hold the breadwinner role in the family. This can lead to a situation where they are having to maintain their own children but do so without some of the more attractive benefits of being a parent. Moreover, when being a breadwinner means that in effect you are maintaining two families, the resultant reduction in standards of living can at times make the whole thing seem less than worthwhile.

Finally, many stepfathers consider that their position in the family is always one of being stuck 'in the middle'. Men who are stepfathers can feel they straddle a position between two women – their current and ex-partner – or between their own children and their new partner. The demands from both sides can make their situation very untenable indeed. Furthermore, if being the focus of competing demands in this way were not enough, stepfathers can also experience the very opposite of this, that is, of being an outsider. Although this is certainly not uniquely a stepfather problem, the solidarity of mother and children can form a disheartening exclusion zone. This can be aggravated by the stepfather's absence from the family home which, as I have indicated, is most often cited as the reason for stepfathers having the easier situation. Who said it was simple being a stepfather?

The purpose of this chapter is to consider these issues in depth. I plan to do this by:

- looking at the position of men in our society;
- focusing on what it means to be a father and a stepfather.

I bring the same perspective to this chapter as I have to the previous one on stepmothers. That is, that you cannot understand the tensions and problems of your situation unless you relate this to the expectations society has of you as a father and stepfather. We begin this process by looking at the recent pressures that men have been experiencing to be more caring and more sensitive.

THE ATTACK ON MEN

There are many pressures on men these days to be more responsive to their partner's and children's needs. No longer will it suffice for them to bring home the wage packet, hand over the housekeeping and disappear to the pub. More is expected of them. They must be caring, sensitive, communicative and, more importantly, share the child-rearing task. As Philip Hodson in his book *Men* points out, there has indeed been a general attack on men in the last twenty-five years. Women have been liberated by the contraceptive pill and technology in the home and are not so tied to the kitchen sink and incessant child-rearing. They have also found their voice, partly through the women's movement, and can now articulate their needs and demands in a public way. Men's responses to these demands appear to fall into one of three modes:

- they counter-attack through men's liberationist tendencies;
- they reaffirm their conventional role through traditionalist tactics;
- they agree there is some benefit in the things women want and attempt the path of becoming the New Man.

MEN'S LIBERATION

It appears that men have experienced many of women's calls for a new deal as a stick to beat them into submission. Their experience is that women are shouting at them and criticising them without appreciating that a man's life is no bed of roses either. For example, men have little choice but to spend their lives in paid work or feel totally inadequate if unemployed. Women, on the other hand, have the benefit of a more punctuated life history, interspaced with caring for a family and being engaged in paid work. Given that work experience for many men is tedious, repetitive and boring, who has the better deal? Men's groups, such as the UK organisation Families Need Fathers, have been formed as a response to what they see as this innate unfairness towards them. This group argues that custody arrangements which favour women and write out men need to be challenged. Indeed, many men feel bitter not only about custody issues but about the whole issue of maintenance. It is men who end up in the bedsitter whilst the ex-partner keeps the marital home. Insult to injury is added when your ex-partner's new lover then moves into your former abode.

TRADITIONALIST TACTICS

Tangential to arguing for men's liberation, men's responses to women's demands for a new deal have also been to seek to reinforce orthodox male/female relationships. We can witness these kinds of responses in the recent debate in Britain about women being allowed to become priests in the Church of England, and in arguments that women should leave the labour force to make way for unemployed men. Conventional relationships between men and women rely on men being providers and women being homemakers. Men occupy the public sphere and women the private. Traditionalists would suggest that this is only right and proper and to live your life in any other way is distinctly unnatural. Underlying these responses is the view, as Philip Hodson puts it, that such men believe that what is good for women is bad for men and traditional men do not defer to women's judgements anyway!

THE NEW MAN

There is, furthermore, a third response. Some men have attempted to respond to women's needs by accepting either that women are indeed equal to men, or that there is some benefit to men in being allowed to move away from the stereotyped macho image. Here the concept of the New Man encompasses the idea that men do indeed have a caring side to their nature. The New Man is supportive of his partner's needs, he takes equal responsibility for the housework and childcare and he is not afraid to show his feelings. The New Man liberates men from having to keep a stiff upper lip and he represents more equality between the sexes.

ACTIVITY

What type of man are you?

Try this quiz. Tick the answer that most closely represents what you think.

	A Agree	B Maybe	C Disagree

1 A woman at work is a man out of work.
2 Men should be able to take on a housewife's role.
3 Maintenance orders should work both ways.
4 Men should never cry.
5 The state should pay for child maintenance.
6 A woman's place is in the home.
7 Couples should have a joint bank account.
8 Children are better off living with their mothers.
9 A wife should not know what her partner earns.
10 Housework should be shared.

Scoring
Score 3 for every A
Score 2 for every B
Score 1 for every C
Points: 1–10   Did you know? You're a New Man!
          11–20 I'm sure you knew. You're a Men's Liberationist!
          21–30 There was never any doubt. You're a Male Traditionalist!

This is an important activity. It will help you to:

- assess what you see is an appropriate way for men to act;
- tell you something about the way you feel family life should be organised.

ACTION

Are you getting a bad deal? Think of a current problem you are experiencing. How do you deal with this problem? The following questions may help you think through some of the ways you could change your approach to the problem:

- Do you want to change?
- Do you keep your feelings to yourself?
- Do you feel ineffective in your step/father role?
- Can the roles of men and women be more interchangeable both in the home and in the workplace?

BEING A FATHER

Has fatherhood changed this century? We have touched a little on the idea that the 1990s has heralded the New Man as the epitome of the caring and sharing male. In particular the New Man puts parenting as an important priority in his life. How is this approach to manhood faring in creating a more equal division of the household labour? Let us consider how the expectations placed on men to be good fathers can shape your experiences. These expectations are:

- sharing the household labour;
- spending time with children;
- being a breadwinner.

You may not be surprised to learn that when it comes to household chores women continue to take the main responsibility. There certainly appear to be preferences, from the man's viewpoint, about the type of housework they like to tackle. Research indicates that men will do the washing up and shopping but are less keen on organising clothes for washing and doing the vacuuming. Yet men do appear to be spending time with their children. They often see this as important to give their wives a chance to get some uninterrupted time to, say, cook an evening meal.

When it comes to the more mundane childcare chores, many men still absent themselves. Research indicates that men continue to have very little to do with bathing babies or changing nappies despite the New Man television advertising! However, father involvement tends to increase as children get older, principally because the children become more like playmates and less dependent on the intense care and servicing demands of babyhood. You can take your three-year-old toddler out to kick a football. Your three-month-old, though, needs a feed, a burp and a change! For many men this still remains women's work.

There is one responsibility, however, that men have always had and continue to have, to be the breadwinner. The demands made on men to build a career or to make up the loss of their wife's earnings after the birth of a child can therefore result in their having to spend longer hours at work. Much research has shown that the timing of a first child matches the time when men's careers are beginning to take off. Rather than being able to share parenting, many fathers actually become less available than ever before. It's a Catch 22 situation. You may want to spend longer with your family but the need to keep a roof over your head and food in your stomach limits this entirely. Moreover, the insecurity of employment facing many people in work today adds even greater incentive to spend long periods of time at work. Your security may depend on showing you are a company person in this kind of way.

None of this is to say that men do not want desperately to build a relationship with their children. In particular, as Charlie Lewis comments in his book *Becoming a Father*, men want to be a playmate for their children. They feel this is an appropriate role for them and feel comfortable doing so. They are also aware that the limited time they have with their children could be jeopardised if they became the disciplinarian in the family. Charlie Lewis's research indicates that fathers tend to be more indulgent with their children than their wives, much to the latter's chagrin! Perhaps here there has been a change to the 'Wait till your father gets home' scenario.

This suggests that men's perspective of their relationship with their children has been changing. Rather than being the distant, authoritative figure, many fathers seek a closer and more rewarding role. However, there can be limitations about the extent to which men are able, despite their own preferences, to be in a position to have such a close relationship. The need to earn the daily bread is one. Another is the way separation and divorce usually mean that the father leaves the family.

THE DIVORCED FATHER

Philip Hodson, in his book *Men*, says quite forthrightly that you can never divorce children. Fatherhood is not an optional extra and it is heretical to consider that it is. Yet statistics indicate that many men after divorce do indeed lose touch with their children, becoming a remote figure symbolised by the Christmas and birthday card which act as a reminder that you do still exist. There can be many reasons for this loosening of ties:

- ideas that mothers are more important to children than fathers;
- vulnerable ties with a child because you no longer live with them;
- bitterness after a divorce;
- time.

Social attitudes, reflected in court decisions that award custody to mothers, exclude fathers from the outset as having no purpose beyond financial maintenance. The desire for a clean break can therefore be confirmed by these post-divorce childcare arrangements. When access visits only bring tension, tears, arguments and the repeated pain of parting, depression sets in. How can one keep a positive and cheerful relationship going when one of its key features is saying goodbye time and time again to a beloved child? As one divorced father I know put it, 'Every week it's like my wife and kids leaving me again.'

In addition, where relationships between father and child were not very strong in the first place, there may be no infrastructure on which to build a continuing one. It is far more difficult maintaining any relationship, let alone a meaningful one, when you do not have the daily rubbing together and sharing which is part and parcel of family life. What fulfilment is there in being the person who takes a child swimming, to the pictures or the zoo but doesn't get to share the intimacy of tucking up their child in bed every night? Over time, the realisation that you are not an integral feature of your child's life loosens even more what may have been fragile bonds in the first place.

When divorce has been bitter, creating distance can also be one way of coping. It may even seem for many fathers that they are doing their children a favour by getting out of their lives. Here the access visit rekindles, in its starkest form, the very features which caused the break-up in the first place. Moreover, it can be that fathers do not feel very much wanted and needed in any case. In fact, is this so surprising when you consider the evidence above that few men really share fully all the domestic tasks and are not so integrated in family life? The need to earn a living means fathers spend much of their time absent so children become dependent on their mother and seemingly less so on their father. Such a vicious circle allows the father legitimately to consider that he is not an essential part of his children's lives.

Finally, it appears from research that time is also a factor. Many fathers initially remain in contact with their children, but one American study indicated that as many as 40% of children no longer saw their father after divorce. Remarriage, of both or either partner, can make contact more and more difficult as the picture becomes complicated by the needs and competing demands of other adults and children. New partners and ex-partners have difficulty getting on, natural children and stepchildren create new rivalries. Eventually the father either gives up in despair or finds the relationship with his own children formal and stifling or traumatic and painful. A move of job or house often provides the catalyst. You really do end up as simply a name on the proverbial Christmas card.

CHILDREN REALLY DO NEED FATHERS

Whilst fathers may find themselves distanced from their children, evidence of children's needs after divorce highlight how important fathers are to their children's well-being. The importance of fathers is confirmed in two ways:

- through psychological theories which now suggest fatherhood has a deeper meaning than purely ensuring a child develops the right sexual identity;
- from children's own views.

The changing expectations of fatherhood we have just considered have been in part paralleled by understandings about the importance of the father to a child's development. Particularly since the Second World War, much of the work in psychology has focused on the mother–child relationship. This was seen to be the paramount relationship in ensuring a child's healthy psychological development. Academic scholarship in this area, particularly arising from feminist-inspired work, has been vocal in its criticism of this. These criticisms have highlighted the way that such theories can pressurise women into a position where they see no alternative in life but to fulfil this idealised function of the perfect mother or end up being blamed for all their children's failings. Consequently, the question has been asked, 'Where does the father figure in all of this?'

The answer, following Freudian analysis, had hitherto been that he is important in helping his children assert their sexual identity but otherwise has little function in a child's development. Interestingly it has been work on what happens to the father-child relationship after divorce that has prompted some rethinking in this area. Wallerstein and Blakeslee's findings, in *Second Chances*, show how fathers remain present, at least psychologically if not physically, in their children's lives. Children need fathers as they do mothers. Wallerstein and Blakeslee argue that they need them because fathers are a crucial factor in forming their child's self-esteem, aspirations and relationships with the opposite sex. An absent father diminishes the child's ability to consider him- or herself a worthwhile person.

Unfortunately, it appears that many fathers simply do not know that children experience the ending of a marriage and the usual consequence of a father leaving as a rejection of themselves. What have I done, the child asks, to make my father leave? As one child put it, 'I thought that I must be a very horrible person if he didn't love me enough to stay with me.'

Wallerstein and Blakeslee further comment how intense this need is. The children in their study showed that they found it intolerable to be separated from their father after divorce whether the father had been good, bad or indifferent. Yet fathers are not aware that their departure causes such sorrow. Research here suggests that whilst fathers think their children are coping, the children themselves experience it in a more traumatic way. Access visits can be one area where this trauma is lived out. The child is excited yet anxious about the visit. Will he turn up? If he doesn't, the notional rejection becomes intensely real. Can I say what I like and don't like without upsetting him? If I upset him, will he come back again? Will I therefore have caused another rejection? And so the thoughts go on.

What may be good news for the absent father is that the quantity of visits count for less than the quality. It would appear that children are well able to understand that a parent cannot visit that often if, say, they live a long distance away although the same is not true if the parent lives close by. In this case there is no excuse for not visiting and when this happens it is often interpreted by the child as a sign that their father does not care about them. However, according to

Wallerstein and Blakeslee, what really counts is that the child feels loved and wanted. It is the quality of the relationship in this respect that matters above all else.

Considering life from the child's point of view is something that perhaps many fathers do not find easy. As we saw in the previous chapter, many women instinctively put their own needs last. For men, you often come first. Yet contrary to much traditional thought, there is evidence that fathers can be just as nurturing as mothers. Just watch a father with his new-born child to see this for yourself. The problem, as Phillip Hodson points out, is that the conditioning men receive to be competitive and to win does not transfer well to the family arena. Here, one thing you can be sure of is that you are more likely to experience failure than success, as any parent will tell you. Children have a knack of going their own way despite your best efforts. The challenge is to be nurturing in a context which supports your masculine self-esteem, rather than seeing it as something which is essentially feminine. It is often the negative associations with 'women's work' which prevent many men from engaging with their children in this way. Yet to do so can give you access to those previously unpermitted feelings of tenderness and emotion.

The deeper challenge for the divorced father is how do I accomplish a fulfilling relationship for my child within the rigours of the access visit? The following activity is designed to enable you to consider the style of your interaction with your children. Often we do things because 'that's the way we've always done it'. What you can ask, however, is whether this meets the different needs of your child: to spend time alone with you, to feel part of a family – even a new one, to enjoy special occasions and have special memories, to stop getting bored, just to know you're there.

ACTIVITY

What kind of time do you spend with your children?

Below are some examples of different types of activity. They are split into categories to indicate the kind of need they will fulfil. Tick the ones you have done with your child/ren in the past twelve months.

Developing a one-to-one relationship:
Hobbies (playing or watching): football, golf, snooker, rugby, squash, darts, pool, horse-riding, tennis, fishing, cars, cricket, bowling, swimming, cinema, chess, stamp collecting

Spending time alone with individual children:
Helping with homework
Shopping for clothes

Being part of a family:
Walking, caravanning, watching television, swimming, cinema, theatre
Staying overnight or for holidays
Sharing a family meal
Visiting relatives

Special occasions:
Birthdays, Christmas, Easter, parties
Creating your own special occasion

Being there:
Phoning to say goodnight
Writing letters
Doing that task they keep nagging you about – like mending a bike, fixing the broken toy
Telling your child you love them

Assessment:
Add up the ticks you have in each category.
Are they roughly in proportion or very out of proportion in each category?
Look to achieve some balance across the activities you engage in.
Do you have some categories with no ticks?
These may be activities you should think of engaging in to create balance in your relationship.

This is an important activity. It will help you:

- gauge where most of your efforts go through access visits;
- look for areas where you could make changes.

This activity should give you an assessment of the type of quality time you spend with your children. It may also help you gauge the likely boredom factor in your routines! Another answer to this dilemma is to talk to your children – ask them how they are coping with their changed circumstances. They may appreciate being consulted.

Remember: Quantity counts but quality counts more.

BEING A STEPFATHER

Within our society, being a father is less determined than being a mother. Moreover, as we have considered, ideas about being a father may be undergoing some change, away from being solely a breadwinner to incorporating a more caring role. This creates difficulties for the stepfather. Without clear boundaries and definitions of what makes a father, the stepfather role is even more diffuse. Should he be a breadwinner, an authoritarian figure, a playmate? Should he be an equal partner in the raising of children, sharing the onerous tasks of childcare and housework? Or should he focus solely on being a partner to his stepchildren's mother and leave the child-rearing to her? After all, they are her children. Add the complication that the stepfather is often a father in his own right and the picture is even more perplexing. As we shall see, any of these responses has benefits and disadvantages. Let us examine this in relation to the stepfather as stepprovider and the stepfather as disciplinarian.

Stepfather or Stepprovider?

Being the breadwinner is certainly a traditional role for a man. Indeed, bringing home the weekly wage vests the man with an authority which is associated with his earning capacity. This is one of the reasons why men historically were given pride of place in the family. Its very survival depended on ensuring that the father was well fed and healthy. If not, only the Poor House awaited. Consequently, most of the family's resources were devoted to giving him the best food and ensuring that he was comfortable. In the stepfamily, however, the stepfather's role as provider can be undermined or can give rise to its own special problems. For example:

- What are the implications when the natural father continues to contribute to the family's finances?
- What are the implications when the natural father does not contribute to the family's finances?
- Does the stepfather expect a 'pay back' for his financial input into the family?

One of the problems confronting the stepfather is that his natural authority as breadwinner can be diminished if the natural father continues to contribute to the upkeep of his children. Where does this leave the stepfather? Happy that he doesn't have the onerous job of working to keep another man's children? Or disgruntled that another man continues to exert the control that comes along with being the paymaster? These questions of finance can leave the stepfather with either no tangible role to play or with the unanticipated penalties of being the main provider.

One area where this can have a resounding effect is in the relationship the stepfather has with his new partner. The receipt of maintenance can give women an independent source of income which may or may not be welcomed by the stepfather. You may feel that this money is not used in the best way for the family as a whole. This can happen particularly where such monies are allocated only to the benefit of the children for whom they are notionally paid. Stepfamilies are notoriously prone to financial problems. They are normally larger than average families as they can include children of two previous marriages and children of the present marriage. The money coming into the house therefore has to go that much further. It doesn't take much imagination to understand the competing tensions between spending maintenance money on the maintenance of the said children or using it to the benefit of the whole family. For men who are used to having the major say in financial affairs, the maintenance monies, over which they have no control, can be particularly galling.

Money coming into the household from another source can also make stepfathers feel that their capacity to be a 'proper' father to their own children is reduced. One stepfather in my own research study used to feel quite resentful at his stepchildren's father. His stepchildren were living full-time with him and their mother and he also had his own children from his first marriage living full-time with him. The father of his stepchildren was pretty well off and would buy them expensive clothes and toys. During the holidays, he could afford to take them abroad. The stepfather felt resentful that he could not afford to do the same thing for his own children and annoyed that his own earning power was not equal to this man's. He also, importantly, felt angry on behalf of his children, that they had to live with the injustice of it. How would you like the stepbrother with whom you live to be walking round in designer trainers when you had to make do with the high-street store's own brand? Especially when he's just returned from a month in the States whilst you had a rainy week camping at Bognor? This kind of situation is excellent for creating sibling rivalry but not so good for creating a peaceful co-existence. It makes it hard to abide by the rule of stepfamily living, that all children should be treated equally.

Of course, in stepfamilies we also very frequently get the very opposite of this situation, when either no maintenance is received or it is insufficient to cover the true costs of keeping children. This is, in fact, probably the most usual circumstance. In this situation the stepfather's resentment is focused on the fact that he is having to keep another man's children. One of the clear responsibilities of fatherhood, now underwritten, in Britain, in the 1991 Child Support Act, is that of financial maintenance. How do you feel, therefore, if your stepchildren's father doesn't abide by his responsibilities? One stepfather I know saw himself as having to take on all the duties of fatherhood and he felt angry at having to do so. In particular, he would point out how he did more for his stepsons than their father had. He was the one who earned the money to pay for their school uniforms, bought them their birthday and Christmas presents, replaced their shoes when they had worn out. He was also the taxi-driver who ferried them about the town, who turned out on cold winter nights to fetch them from friends' houses. Not only was he the financial provider but he was also the mainstay of their lives. He felt quite indignant. Here he was keeping them, with his whole life put out by it, with no thanks, no reward.

Unfortunately stepchildren are very unresponsive to the emotional needs of their stepparents (not just stepfathers). This may be because of the commitment such children have to their natural parent. Wallerstein and Blakeslee, in their book *Second Chances*, make this point very forcibly. They say that the stepfather relationship can never be the same as the relationship between child and biological father. Stepfathers who try to make it so are bound to fail. The emotional commitment children have to their father is good news for dads, but not so good for stepfathers, especially as we all need some recompense for our generosity!

One area where stepfathers might seek such gratification is through their stepchildren taking their surname. We live in a society that still takes it almost for granted that on marriage the new wife will take her husband's name. Husbands do not normally take their new wife's name. This convention can create a sense of ownership and belonging. There is a lot of social and psychological investment in a name. Fathers often want a son to carry on the family name. Their dynastic aspirations rely on this to happen.

As well as these traditional issues, names in a stepfamily can create all sorts of hassle. Stepchildren who retain their father's name can have a mother who takes her new partner's name on remarriage. This causes all sorts of confusion when dealing with the various aspects of officialdom – schools, doctors, social security and so on. It also repeatedly exposes your whole family history to the inevitable looks and questions which arise. Don't you get fed up with explaining that this child's surname is not the same as yours because she is a stepchild but this child's surname is because he is your natural child? Whose business is it anyway? Consequently, to get rid of this unwelcome intrusiveness into your private life it might seem much easier to change all the children's names to yours. However, whilst logic may dictate such action as appropriate, there is still a lot of emotive attachment in a name. The emotive issue will outrule the logic every time.

Harry Johnson, a stepfather I know very well, still gets very upset at the fact that his stepson, Adam Williams, did not want to change his surname. His stepson is now in his mid-twenties and works in the same business as Harry. From time to time people who do not know the family history assume they are father and son. This means that Harry is sometimes called Mr Williams by mistake, and likewise Adam gets called Mr Johnson occasionally. Harry is either left to explain that he is Mr Johnson, and not Adam's natural father, or to leave the mistake which causes ongoing confusion and misidentity. But it isn't so much this confusion that upsets Harry. It's the fact that Adam has always insisted on retaining his father's name, even though he hasn't seen his own father for ten years. Harry sees this as a rejection of him as a parent. Whilst Harry has been a father in everything but name, Adam does not acknowledge this through the taking of his name.

However, Harry does not share this feeling of rebuttal with Adam. No, he keeps this stoically to himself. How could he expose this almost unallowed feeling of wanting a very concrete sign of being accepted? What he does get angry about publicly, though, are more tangible issues. Adam comes to dinner every Saturday evening. After dinner, Adam's mother fills a bag full of leftovers and other goodies – food, wine, beer plus the odd £10 note. She's doing nothing more than most mums do. But this is a stepfamily remember and Harry has paid for all these items. And the £10 note was the very one he gave his wife the day before! Yet he sees these trophies carried off by the boy who has refused the ultimate accolade of taking his name. 'I paid for all that,' shouts Harry. 'Why should he still continue to live off me?' Indeed, why should he?

Whilst some stepfathers resent being the stepprovider, others positively welcome it. They perceive the power of the moneybox as giving them the ultimate power in the family. Another stepfather I know, Tom, tried to limit every attempt by his stepchildren's father to have contact with them – both financially and through access visits. In fact, no access visits were allowed. Tom saw to that. He was also very pleased that the father made no payments to the family. It was his proof that he was the better man. The natural father did, however, continue to send Christmas and birthday gifts. Tom found these very unwelcome reminders that there was a real father out there somewhere, who had not totally forgotten his children. Tom would get quite irritable when these presents arrived. They were a potent effigy of previous relationships he did not want to acknowledge. Tom's way of coping was to dismiss the gifts as paltry and he would describe them as cheap plastic rubbish. His glee was evident when his stepchildren treated them as rubbish and his accounts were joyful of the way that the children dumped their father's presents in preference for the ones that he had purchased. Needless to say, he had also ensured that these children carried his surname. You could say, all in all, that Tom's masculine dominance was well asserted in all spheres of this stepfamily's life! Rule the roost he certainly did. Let's have a look at this in a little more detail.

THE AUTHORITARIAN STEPFATHER

Spare the rod, spoil the child so the old saying goes. Is this the stepfather's motto? When you are unsure of what your position is in the stepfamily, the disciplinarian is at least a clearly identifiable role. Don't be deceived though. Discipline can be as confusing an issue in the stepfamily as in any other. Here we consider two aspects of the matter:

- authority as seen as an appropriate masculine role;
- but how appropriate in the stepfamily?

Being the disciplinarian would certainly fit with a traditional role for men when they become stepfathers. The stern Victorian father is the role model for this behaviour. After all, it is so identifiable with what we suppose makes a good father. It is also a position which is seen to be complementary to the mother. Where the mother is soft, pliable, dare we say weak, the father is strong, assertive, in control and hard. Furthermore, these character traits are just the elements of masculinity heralded as appropriate for being a real man. So, where it is difficult to find any tangible role for oneself, the authoritarian stepfather provides an easy answer.

In addition, stepfathers are not hampered by fears of being perceived to be wicked in the way that stepmothers are. The stepfather is more likely to be viewed as a knight in shining armour come to rescue a distressed mother and her deserted children rather than someone come to render evil and abuse. In the area of discipline, stepfathers are accordingly free from any automatic negative associations about their behaviour. They have a headstart compared to stepmothers. Strictness and authority are seen as an admirable strength, without any strings attached.

Research indicates that many stepfathers do indeed see their role as making up for the deficiencies of mothers in the areas of discipline and order in their homes. The mother's job is to bring the children up, the stepfather's to ensure that she does this properly. Many couples find that this can be a significant area of disagreement. As one stepfather said:

'I saw it that it was up to me to keep order. Their mother was hopeless. She let them do as they pleased and they never listened to her if she told them off. When they lived alone they got used to doing just what

**they wanted. When I came all that had to change. But
she didn't see it that way. She thought I was trying to
take over. All I was doing was trying to get some order
out of chaos. Get them to give her some respect.'**

The ensuing disagreements developed into personal slanging
matches between the adults; 'You're a lousy mother' versus
'You're a belligerent stepfather' with the odd 'They're selfish
kids' thrown in. At this stage you're in a cycle that is hard to
climb out of. These personal elements neglect the fact that
your disagreements are often the result of the situation you
are in, rather than the personalities involved. Scenes of this
kind are replicated throughout stepfamilies every day of the
year. Either we have to accept the fact that the world is
populated by lousy mothers and insensitive stepfathers
thrown mercilessly together at random or there are some
independent features of the stepfamily situation that is the
cause of this debâcle.

We have already considered that taking on the mantle of
authority in a stepfamily is an appropriate masculine role. It
upholds ideas of decent male behaviour and at least gives
you an identity you can hang on to within the volatile
pressures of stepfamily life. It is also one way in which you
can show that you care in a fitting way. One of the stepfathers
in my own research study, Paul, certainly saw the reason for
his disciplinary behaviour to be just this. He spoke at length
about the need to show who is in charge in the family. For
him it was his way of maintaining his hereditary authority. 'If
a man can't be boss of his house where can he be the boss?'
would probably sum up this type of attitude. Paul had no
fears about using physical punishment as a way of maintaining control. He would talk about 'coming the hard and heavy'
on his stepchildren and maintain that this was essential
because it shows that you care. Unfortunately, I'm not
convinced that being on the receiving end of a punishing
adult would be much of a sign that I was cared for. Are you?

It appears to me that such men are trapped by behaving in
ways which appear appropriate as a role model in the wider

society but which are totally inappropriate within the realities of family life. Authority comes in many guises. It can arise from some kind of charisma which the person in charge has. We have all heard of the type of leader whose followers would go with them to the ends of the earth just because of the strength of their personality. This person has a charismatic power that is hard to resist. There is authority that arises from brute force. The regimes of inhumanity in many totalitarian states would be a good analogy. Here people follow out of terror and obey out of fear. And then there is the authority that is earned. Democracies argue that this is the basis of their power; it is earned through the ballot-box if not through their practice and policies! Stepfathers who believe that they have an automatic right to be the disciplinarian are operating on the basis of the totalitarian state. It is power wrested from the inhabitants not power earned through respect and hard work. What right does anyone entering a family have to assume, by virtue of their sex, that they should be the one in charge? Unfortunately, many men are taught that they have that place by right.

When we add the potent force of children's discontent to this recipe we can see how many of the problems arise. Traditionally children inhabit a position within society where they have to obey the dictates of adults. This is much the same at school, for example, as within the family. The stepfather here, however, is on very slippery ground. Whilst children may, just, give credence to their teacher's wishes by virtue of the authority that stems from that role, you as stepfather don't have a legitimate role in their eyes. They already have a father. As far as they're concerned, if they are going to listen to anyone, it will be him. Your status as a stepfather is, in consequence, a non-status. You have no more innate power or authority than the next-door neighbour. They can choose whether or not to listen to him in just the same way as they may choose to listen to you.

In your eyes, however, not only do you carry the authority that is the prerogative of masculinity but you are also living with them and keeping them. Surely that gives you some rights. Probably, but not till you've earned it. This is why all advice books on the stepfamily tell stepfathers to take the discipline issue slowly. They are telling you that you have to earn your 'democratic' authority not charge in like Ghengis Khan annihilating all opposition in the process. When you take the latter course you are destined for trouble. Your stepchildren will organise a resistance which will resonate through every aspect of your private life. That's why people often describe the disagreements in stepfamilies as being like the Second World War breaking out. Our society may stereotype children into the subordinate role. It's a mistake to believe the propaganda though. We all know that subordinates strive to be superordinates. Children are no exception. Many stepparents would say stepchildren especially so!

The following activity is designed to enable you to assess your approach to discipline. The activity is designed to include an assessment of your approach to your stepchildren, your children (if any) from a first marriage and any 'our' children you may have. The reason for this is that often children perceive that they are being particularly unfairly treated when it comes to discipline, when compared to step or half-siblings. The activity should highlight if you are inadvertently acting in this way. In addition, the activity makes a distinction between male and female children to draw out any distinctions in your approach here.

ACTIVITY

How do you discipline?

Put a tick in the correct space according to the disciplinary approach you have used.

	YOUR KIDS		HER KIDS		OUR KIDS	
	Boy	Girl	Boy	Girl	Boy	Girl
Physical smack						
Shout						
Ignore						
Send to room						
Placing sanctions on child (grounded, no sweets, etc)						
Discuss the 'problem'						
Make a short statement to show your displeasure						
Nag						
Lecture						

Assessment
Look at the pattern of your ticks. It will tell its own story.

This is an important activity. It will help you:

- see if there is any difference in the way you discipline individual children;
- show if you have a preferred style.

Remember: All the worthwhile things in life have to be earned. Authority is one of them.

We have so far explored in depth some of the problems confronting men in their stepparenting of other people's children. In particular, we have looked at the stereotypes of male behaviour and considered how they work in stepfamily life. Our final step to successful stepfatherhood is to look at an issue which is very probably close to your heart. This is the impossibility of being stuck in the middle of someone else's war.

PIGGY IN THE MIDDLE

We've all played the children's game piggy in the middle. It's fun when you're six, isn't it? But it's not much fun when you're thirty-six or forty-six. Unfortunately, it seems to go with being an adult male in a stepfamily. How many times have you felt that you were part of the ping-pong between either your current partner and your ex or between your children and their stepmother? I know. I've often put my husband in the same situation. It's a no-win situation for you, torn apart by wanting to satisfy everyone. The impossibility of that means that you get it in the neck from all sides.

Now I'm aware that I'm preaching to the converted here, in the sense that you would like to see an end to this behaviour. This is why I've included some commentary about this issue in the previous chapter on stepmotherhood. Stepmothers may not be so converted to seeing the necessity for change as you are and it is for this reason that I felt it was important to deal with this issue at that point. One of the ways that stepmothers use their partners is as a disciplinarian of their stepchildren. They do this for various reasons, one of which is so that they themselves do not have to behave in ways which might make them act like the Wicked Stepmother. And disciplining stepchildren in their view can appear that way.

However, on the assumption that it takes two to make or break a relationship, stand by for the second attack directed at you! The objective here is to get beyond the personal investment we have in our own problems and to see the situation with a little more detachment. I plan to put the stepmother's case before you. Yes, I know you've heard it from your partner hundreds of times before. But if anything I say comes near to what she has to say, perhaps you will see how common the problem is. And thereby see that it's not a personal attack on your inadequacies but an inevitable tension of stepfamily life. So here goes.

What do women want? An age-old cry from men, I know, and one you have uttered a thousand times. What does she want from me? I hear you say. You work hard and have no vices. If you went off with other women or gambled away the equity on the house, well, maybe she'd have something to gripe about. As it is, the only thing you can think you haven't done is mended the leak in the roof. And it's not raining so what's the worry? So what does she want? I can tell you in one short word – commitment. No, not the commitment of the wedding ring and having babies, although that may be an issue in your life. The kind of commitment I'm talking about here is more mundane than that, more integral to the whole of your relationship, more implicit than explicit. It's a commitment that tells your partner that you are on her side, that you are supporting her – whether she's right or wrong. It comes from your automatic, unthought behaviour, not from the more self-conscious things you do that show you care. This is probably why it's so hard to work out. It's wonderful to receive flowers, to be taken out for a special meal. But without the unspoken commitments that form the bedrock of a relationship, these gestures are like islands in the sea. Unfortunately, for many women living in stepfamilies, the islands are too far apart and the sea is turbulent and full of sharks.

One regular example of piggy in the middle occurs when stepmother and stepchild disagree. Both are vying for you to side with them. What is your response? Absolute self-preservation. You do nothing. The result? Both sides are angry with you because neither is victorious. You're in trouble. What both sides want is your support. Whilst, as far as you're concerned, you've stayed neutral, in their eyes you've failed to offer that support. That is tantamount to betrayal. Listen to this stepmother. Her words are very common in this situation.

> 'Janice [stepdaughter] started shouting at me. Telling me she hated me. That I was a vile stepmother. He [husband] didn't say anything. He sat there and listened! He never once told her not to speak to me like that. To give me a bit of respect. I couldn't speak to him for days. How could he treat me like that?

So the stepmother's disagreement with her stepdaughter becomes focused on you. Your silence here is interpreted by your partner not as neutrality but as support for your child – her stepchild. And in times of anger the stepchild is usually defined as the enemy. Your silence is also interpreted as a sign that you don't really care about your partner. Here all kinds of thoughts get mixed up. Your partner thinks you care more for your child than her, therefore, illogically, you really care more for your first partner than her. And so on. Not the stuff of good marital relationships, is it?

So what do you do? Especially when you actually do agree with your own child's point of view but the politics of your marriage suggest you just keep quiet? Try following the rules set out below. You may no longer find yourself piggy in the middle!

ACTIVITY

Rules for a peaceful life

Rule No. 1: As all books on parenting dictate – at least in public, father and mother must support each other. Children rapidly see a chink in the armour they can exploit, if not. In stepfamilies this rule is even more important. The stepmother is similar to the stepfather here in that she does not have the natural authority of a mother. She has to earn it and work hard for it. Stepchildren and their fathers siding with each other make this impossible.

Rule No. 2: Talk to your wife about how you feel. Let her know, in as supportive a way possible, that you don't like being asked to intervene in rows between her and your children or to discipline them on her behalf. Get her to read Chapter Two of this book.

Rule No. 3: Talk to your children about how you feel. Let them know, in as supportive a way possible, that you won't intervene in rows between them and their stepmother but neither will you tolerate certain kinds of behaviour. Get them to read all this book.

Rule No. 4: Try to understand what stepfamily life is like from the viewpoint of all its inhabitants. Read all of this book.

Remember: Sitting on the fence is interpreted as betrayal. Fence-sitters beware.

REVIEW

The key messages of this chapter are:

- stepfathers can also be non-custodial fathers of their own children. This can make their situation doubly difficult;
- stepfathers do not have a clear role in the stepfamily;
- the traditional male roles of provider and disciplinarian work differently in a stepfamily situation;
- discipline should be approached with care;
- commitment is at the centre of the problem of being piggy in the middle

Remember: Superheroes need love, tolerance, dependability and understanding. So do stepfathers.

4

Positive parenting

Do you get hot under the collar at the mere mention of a stepchild's name? Do you feel your hackles rise, your pulse rate quicken, your stomach churn? When you think of your relationship with your stepchild, do you hang your head in shame, experience a nagging sense of guilt, wonder how you failed so abysmally? Do you think your stepchildren are the most ungrateful kids in the world, who take and never give, who have never learnt the words thank you? If so, welcome to stepparenthood. You are a fully fledged member.

Parenting stepchildren is parenting with a plus. You can liken the experience to a race where stepparents start from behind, with their hands tied behind their backs and one leg in plaster. Parenting itself is well acknowledged to be one of the most complex of tasks. Think of all the jobs parents do. They are breadwinners, nurses, bike repairers, counsellors, psychologists, chefs, teachers, taxi drivers, launderers, entertainers. Parenting in the 20th century means helping children avoid the hazards of drug and alcohol abuse; it means supporting their education; it means ensuring their safety. Stepparenting is all of these and more. It is parenting a child who may have conflicting feelings about their circumstances. It is parenting a child who travels between two homes. It is parenting a child who has divided loyalties. It is parenting a child who has, in some way, lost a parent.

That many stepparents and children strive to make their relationships work despite the obstacles in their path is a very strong message from those who live in and work with stepfamilies. It is one that should not be forgotten in the clamour we hear about the effects of bad parenting. We can all too easily focus on the negative and forget the positive. Indeed, as the title of one of the first British books on the stepfamily, by Jackie Burgoyne and David Clarke, indicates many stepfamilies are in fact *Making a Go of It*.

This chapter is all about making stepparenting a positive experience. The focus of the chapter is to look at both sides of the stepparenting relationship, that is, to consider the relationship from the viewpoint of the stepchild and the stepparent. I believe this is the only way that progress can be made. To contribute to this, the chapter asks the following questions:

- What makes a successful stepparent–stepchild relationship?
- What do stepchildren want from stepparents?
- What do stepparents want from stepchildren?

Remember: Successful stepparent–stepchild relationships are common. The problem is, we hear less about their success than others' failure.

LIKELY SUCCESS FACTORS IN STEPPARENT–STEPCHILD RELATIONSHIPS?

What makes a successful stepparent–child relationship? This is the question most often asked by those who seek to understand the dynamics of stepfamily life. We too must ask this question as our first step in creating positive parenting experiences. There are three key areas which have been seen to influence the likely success of stepparent–stepchild relations. These are:

- age;
- sex of child and sex of stepparent;
- whether the stepfamily was formed as a result of divorce or death of a previous partner.

But a word of warning before you proceed. There are few clear agreements about how significant each of these factors are.

AGE

The younger the better, or the older the sooner they will be gone? One of the factors that has been thought to contribute to the likely success of a steprelationship is the age of the child. Unfortunately, there doesn't seem to be a consensus on this. On the one hand, it is argued that the younger the child is when she or he acquires a stepparent, the easier will be the ensuing relationship. This is because the child will be more amenable to the authority of the stepparent and more adaptable to a new parent's expectations and attitudes. On the other hand, Brenda Maddox comments that stepparents themselves would say that the older the child, the better the relationship. Why? Because they have less time to spend in the family home before finding their independence.

Does age make a difference? As I've said, the findings are confusing. What does make a practical difference is the child's maturity and independence. The seven-year-old cannot make his or her own arrangements to see a non-custodial parent. The seventeen-year-old can. My stepson and stepdaughter can now make their own arrangements to see their mother. Thankfully I do not have to be involved. It is one area therefore where my anxieties no longer tip over into my relationship with them.

So the significance of age is that it might tell us something about the needs and demands which are placed upon a stepparent or the extent of involvement stepparents and stepchildren have with each other. But clearly, young or old, these factors can vary immensely.

SEX

Again, the sex of the child is seen to be important in determining the likely quality of a steprelationship. In particular, same sex relationships are seen to be the most difficult. Rivalry between stepfather and stepson and between stepmother and stepdaughter are seen to abound. In fact, it is only in connection with the stepmother–stepdaughter relationship that there appears to be agreement. This relationship is considered to be the least likely to succeed. The reason given is usually some kind of sexual jealousy between stepmother and stepdaughter. The stepdaughter becomes the living image of the first wife and reminds the stepmother of the sexual relationship her partner had before her. Whilst I have no problem in accepting the idea of 'like mother, like daughter' I am not so convinced personally of the relevance of a stepdaughter being a reminder of a previous sexual relationship. Rather, I view it that not many women want to live with their partner's ex, particularly if there is animosity in the relationship, as so often there is. 'Like mother, like daughter' can therefore be a bit like living with that ex. Sexual jealousy or not!

Let me give you another example of why the stepmother–stepdaughter relationship can be so fraught. As we shall consider in the next chapter, one concern for the stepfamily is whether or not to have a baby. This can be an unresolved issue for a long time. For a stepmother with a teenage stepdaughter, her own fears at not having a child can be transferred into fears that her stepdaughter will. In particular, the stepmother pictures being left to care for a stepgrandchild before, or even in place of, having a child of her own. One stepmother I know, Sally, explained to me these anxieties in the context of her stepdaughter's current wayward behaviour.

The stepdaughter, it seemed, had become friendly with a young man who had been in trouble with the police. Sally and her husband had tried to persuade their daughter to end the relationship and had banned the young man from the house. This is perhaps not that unusual in any family. Parents disliking their child's choice of friends is in fact very common. When those friends include people who have engaged in criminal behaviour it is very understandable. Even the ensuing rows are predictable and can be seen as part of the common stock of growing up.

However, the immense distress which Sally was feeling went beyond these concerns. Her distress was underlain by the fact that her stepdaughter might become pregnant. As Sally is still childless, it is perhaps no wonder that she is especially sensitive and vulnerable. Such vulnerability takes the form of argument and bitterness. Let us also not forget that, as the main carer of the family, as we examined in Chapter Two, there is a level of reality in Sally's fears. It is mums and stepmums who are indeed left holding the baby – their own or their step-offspring's.

The message here is that there may be a very tangible reason why a relationship between two members of the same sex is particularly hazardous. If you can find the reason, you may be halfway there to improving a situation.

Death or Divorce

Are you a stepfamily as a result of death or divorce? In the 1990s the predominant reason is divorce, in contrast to the past when divorce was not so easily accessible. Again, there are no conclusive findings as to whether it is death or divorce that gives rise to the more difficult steprelationships. Clearly children experience a tremendous sense of loss and sadness whether their parents have divorced or one has died. Both events require mourning and adjustment. Yet it is argued that death can lead to the deceased parent becoming idealised, a hard act, therefore, for the living and imperfect stepparent to live up to. This argument, however, suggests that the non-custodial parent, in the case of divorce, does not become idealised. However, research findings also indicate that many non-custodial fathers, in particular, soon disappear from their children's lives. Such absent fathers, though still alive, can also easily become idealised.

The argument that divorce makes stepparenting harder is that stepchildren still have a living parent, therefore the stepchild is placed in a situation of divided loyalties. In addition, divorce can bring with it financial problems as houses have to be sold and maintenance paid. This is not to deny that widowhood also brings financial worries. Yet access visits represent constant interruptions to 'normal' life and, as they are a reminder of the past, make it difficult to build a new life free of that past. Where the non-custodial parent showers children with expensive presents and generally spoils them, the full-time carers are left feeling bleak in comparison, and resentful too.

Do the reasons for remarriage make any difference to the success factor of a stepfamily? I doubt very much that we can divide death- or divorce-generated stepfamilies neatly in this kind of way. What matters is how we deal with the situations we face in life. How you recreate your life and relationships after a death or divorce is what counts, rather than only the events which led to how a stepfamily came into being.

WHAT CAN WE LEARN FROM THE AGE, SEX, DEATH, DIVORCE CHARACTERISTICS?

Whilst the picture that emerges about these characteristics is confusing, we should not be too hasty in dismissing their value. At one level these distinctions are indeed useful. They help you:

- see that some of the problems you confront are not due to your defective personality but are inherent in independent factors beyond your control;
- enable you to predict the likelihood, though not the certainty, that you may experience some problems.

Take the example that it is thought that older children are less likely to respond affectionately or positively to a stepparent. This can be important in helping you see the 'It's not just me' factor. If you have experienced problems with older stepchildren, this knowledge should help you take a step back from the situation and know that these problems are not due to your wickedness or austere personality. These situations are common and can indeed be predictable.

The predictability element of these criteria can also help you to assess how problematic your steprelationships are likely to be. As a stepmother with an adolescent stepdaughter, for example, the odds are stacked against your finding this a particularly easy relationship. Marrying a woman whose previous husband had died will tell you that it is possible, even likely, that your stepchildren will build idealised pictures of their natural father. Such knowledge, at a minimum, gives you some forewarning of the kind of problems you are likely to face.

There are drawbacks however about the factors of age, sex and divorce/widowhood. In particular, there is in fact very little you can do about any of them!

You can't change the sex of your stepdaughter, nor the divorce or death of a parent. As regards age, well, older children do leave home but they never stop being a stepchild. Younger children grow older and present all the common problems of growing up and adolescence.

Whilst you cannot change your stepchildren there is another way of tackling any problems you may experience. Try to understand them. This has to be our next step to developing successful stepparent–child relationships. Be warned though. It's a hard step to take.

GETTING TO KNOW YOUR STEPCHILD

How well do you know how your stepchild feels about her or his family circumstances? Rarely do we discuss our innermost feelings with our stepchildren. The risks are too great; you may unearth feelings that might best be hidden. You don't want to hear the bad things. Will you believe the good?

Anyway, I hear you say, we understand them perfectly. What we need is a book for stepchildren telling them to understand us! You're right if you have these thoughts. Too often we berate our own inadequacies and neglect to understand that children can act in equally vile and less than understanding ways.

However, my purpose in asking you to go through this process is not just because it will be good for your soul – though it will be. Rather it is to:

- make clear that there is another point of view;
- present you with an opportunity you should not miss – that is, get to know how your stepchildren might feel through the experiences of other people's stepchildren. This is much less risky.

Hold my hand and take that step. Here is Emma's story, written in her mid-20s but reflecting back to her lost child-hood. Emma was already living in a stepfamily after her mother's divorce from her father when she was two. Her mother remarried and had a son, Emma's half-brother, but left this second marriage when Emma was ten years old. Emma was left to live with her stepfather and, shortly afterwards, her stepmother.

'It seemed at the time that only days had passed from when Mum moved out to when my stepmother moved in. I was devastated by the upheaval in my life, and very angry. My anger was directed towards my stepfather more than my stepmother for the following reasons:

1 he seemed to plunge into another relationship without satisfactorily concluding the first;
2 he gave me no chance to grieve for the loss of my mother from my immediate family circle;
3 he seemed to expect that I carry on as normal with another woman whom I didn't know in the place where my mother had been – in his life and in his bed.
4 Consequently, he seemed to be trampling all over my feelings.

'I was ten years old when my mother went. I think I was quite an "old" ten.
'I felt unimportant and rejected by him and my

mother; he was only interested in his "new woman" and Mum did not seem to want me enough to take me with her when she left, although I knew she couldn't. Most importantly of all, I felt that I no longer had a family, that I was being pushed towards the fringes of everyone's life. After all, I was not his [stepfather's] child, I thought, but the offspring of my mother's in a previous marriage. I had no blood ties to anyone in my "family" – immediate or expanded – except my half-brother, and at the time my half-brother and I did not get on at all, which is a fairly typical occurrence. He was five years old. I felt completely alone and cut off.

'It is not clear now in my mind whether my father prepared me or my half-brother for the coming of a new woman into his life, and ours. I vaguely remember that she visited a few times before she moved in with us. Her personality was very different in comparison to my mother's, which made me wonder if he had ever loved my mother, or me. (I saw myself as an extension of my mother.) She had insisted that my father adopt me before they got married. I kept on asking myself if he had seen me as a necessary extra baggage in order to embark on a relationship with my mother. I resented my stepmother for taking my mother's place in my stepfather's life so quickly (although I would have probably felt the same had the interim period been longer) and I was adamant within myself that she was not a replacement for me. I felt relieved when my stepmother concurred with this, but still I felt insecure and neglected, and afraid that he would throw me out, as I represented a failure in his life: the failure of the relationship between himself and my mother.

'I questioned the motives of my stepmother for wanting to be a part of our lives. Did she just want my stepfather? Did my half-brother and myself figure in their new commitment? Did she actually like either of us, or were we just more necessary extra baggage. Did she love my stepfather? In what way did she see a relationship with my stepfather to be advantageous? Why did she have to change things, from items in the home to the way we celebrated Christmas? Was my stepfather being unfaithful with her before my mother left? Why did she, just by becoming part of our family, make me feel like a spare part, almost a lodger in my own home? If she loved my stepfather, why could she not have waited until my stepfather and mother were totally irreconcilable before she moved in and changed all our lives?

'At the time, I felt she resented me. I was a constant reminder of my stepfather's relationship with my mother. I looked like my mother; acted like her. I felt as if she was jealous of me, and could never understand why, as she had my stepfather now, not my mother, or me, if I ever did have a part of him. I thought that neither of them would listen to my questions, that I was not important enough and they seemed too wrapped up in each other to notice me, or my need for answers.

'I wondered, if my stepparents were adults and therefore reasonable and knowledgeable people:

1 Why did my stepmother wish to blot out any trace of my mother, to the extent of moving house?
2 Why did she and my stepfather make me feel guilty for loving my mother and wanting to see her? The morning of the day when Mum would call to pick up my half-brother and myself was always fraught with tension.
3 Why did my stepmother change so much? First she would be very supportive, then she would hate the sight of me and yell at me for no reason.
4 Why did they hate my mother, and did they hate me too because I was my mother's daughter?
5 Why couldn't they see that I was different; that the bad character aspects that they thought my mother had were not automatically part of my character?'

Is there any chance you have a stepchild who feels this way? Chances are you might. Although Emma's stepfather had brought her up from babyhood and had adopted her, Emma was in a slightly unusual situation to be with two step-parents. Nevertheless, her experiences are borne out by the stories of other children. Let's complete our insight into the life of a stepchild by looking at these.

We shall do this by looking at the key findings of three studies that have been concerned about the lives of children after divorce and when they become stepchildren. These studies are *Second Chances* by Wallerstein and Blakeslee, *Stepchildren: A National Study* by Elsa Ferri and *Children in the Middle* by Ann Mitchell.

We shall look at them individually and then consider their common messages.

RESEARCH STUDY ONE: *SECOND CHANCES* BY WALLERSTEIN AND BLAKESLEE

American researchers Wallerstein and Blakeslee interviewed 116 children ten years after their parents had separated and divorced. The youngest was eleven and the oldest was twenty-nine. Their key findings were:

Children's experiences of divorce:
- Divorce is almost always more devastating for children than their parents.
- The effects of divorce are often long lasting. Children are especially affected because divorce occurs during their formative years.
- Almost all children of divorce regard their childhood and adolescence as having taken place in the shadow of divorce.

For the children, the post-divorce years brought the following:
- Half saw their mother or father get a second divorce in the ten-year period after the first divorce.
- Half grew up in families where parents remained angry with each other.

- One in four children experienced a severe drop in their standard of living.
- Three in five felt rejected by at least one parent, sensing that they were a piece of psychological or economic baggage left over from a regretted journey.
- Many children felt excluded from the remarried family.
- One wonders how, but Wallerstein and Blakeslee report that many children emerged into young adulthood as compassionate, courageous and competent people – helped by supportive relationships of one or both parents, grandparents and stepparents.

In their foreword to the study Wallerstein and Blakeslee comment that we are sometimes too keen to underestimate the potentially damaging effects of divorce, too keen to see these as short term. They comment:

'Of course it is important to note that many of the children in this study did ultimately recover from the trauma and have gone on to live contented and stable adult lives. It is also true that we cannot be certain as to the quality of life of any or all of these children had their parents not divorced at all. Such caveats are important. But they are not so important as to distract us from the central disturbing message of this study which is that there are no grounds for assuming that because divorce can often be very much better for the adults involved it must likewise be good for the children.'

RESEARCH STUDY TWO: *STEPCHILDREN: A NATIONAL STUDY* BY ELSA FERRI

Elsa Ferri's study used data from an ongoing study of 17,000 children who were all born in one week of March 1958. This study, called the National Child Development Study, was set up in 1964 to monitor the educational, social and physical development of these children. Elsa Ferri took a sample of children from this study when they had reached the age of 16, who were living with one natural parent and a stepparent. Her aim was to consider the effects that living in a stepfamily had on these children. There are many caveats attached to the findings of this study which makes it difficult to summarise. Nevertheless some key findings are:

- Children with stepfathers were much more likely than those in unbroken families to have poor relationships with their fathers.
- Children with stepmothers were far less likely to get on well with their mothers than were those with two natural parents.
- Girls in stepfamilies seem to want an early marriage.
- Boys with stepmothers seem reluctant to marry and have children of their own.
- Stepchildren have relatively low aspirations about staying on at school and continuing their studies.

Although Elsa Ferri reminds us that we should assess her findings with caution, she does comment that whilst there was no particular adverse effect for the majority of children being brought up in a stepfamily, there were concerns among a minority of stepchildren that their experiences were not all those we could have wished.

RESEARCH STUDY THREE: *CHILDREN IN THE MIDDLE* BY ANN MITCHELL

Ann Mitchell's work is a study of children living through divorce. She interviewed sixty mothers, eleven fathers and fifty children who were all aged 16–18 at the time of the interview and had been aged 10–13 at the time of divorce. An interesting finding in Ann Mitchell's study was that one-quarter of new partners had been known to the children for many years, for example as a neighbour, or an aunt's divorced husband. Rather than being pleased, however, at a familiar figure joining the family, some children actually resented having to live with someone they had known in a different role. Clearly, familiarity is not necessarily a crucial determinant in the likely success of the stepparent relationship. A further key message from Ann Mitchell's study is that there appears to be a chasm between the parent's perspective and the child's. For example:

- Although parents had often assumed that their children would be happy or accepting at acquiring a stepparent, this wasn't always the case.
- Children's feelings when introduced to a new prospective stepparent were ambiguous. Some resented the idea of having a new parental figure whether known beforehand or not and irrespective of the way they got to know them.
- Children's feelings for their new parental figures ranged from a warm love to a strong resentment; from pleasure at once again being a two-parent family to anger at the introduction of an unwanted newcomer.
- One child in four with a new parental figure in the family home had never liked him or her.
- In general, children had been less appreciative of stepparent figures than their own parents had indicated. Some parents did not seem to have been aware of their children's antipathy to their new partners.
- Non-custodial parents' new partners, i.e. the part-time stepfamily, were seldom looked on as stepparents even when they had married the parents. The new partner was mainly viewed as a friend of their parent. As one child in the study commented, 'I can't have a stepmother because I've still got a mother.'
- On the whole, the children painted a blacker picture of the new parent figures in their homes than might have been expected from their parents' accounts.
- Ann Mitchell's message is, parents can change partners but children cannot change parents. They can gain additional parents. It seems, though, that they don't often like them.

Did you think any of these findings were surprising? Did they make you feel uneasy as you read through them? I know I did when I first read them. I felt that they touched those fears I would prefer to keep suppressed, that, despite my best intentions, some actions do indeed bear adversely on our children.

Although these details have been about someone else's stepchildren, you may find it worthwhile using this material to think about the common problems stepchildren face and your own situation.

ACTIVITY

What do we know about stepchildren?

Complete the boxes

I have learnt from these research studies that step-children are:

The factors I was surprised to learn about stepchildren were:

The factors I was not surprised to learn about step-children were:

This is an important activity. It will help you to:

- take a detached look at the needs of stepchildren;
- understand that stepchildren have their own expectations

and concerns which may not be the same as yours or their natural parents';

● consider how these findings confirm or do not confirm your own understandings about your stepchildren.

Now try a similar exercise in relation to your own personal situation.

ACTIVITY

What do I know about my stepchildren?

The feelings my stepchildren have about the divorce/ death of their parent are: (*you may put different answers for different children*)

The feelings my stepchildren have about living in a stepfamily are: (*you may put different answers for different children*)

In what kinds of ways would you say your stepchildren are better or worse off in a stepfamily?

This is an important activity. It will help to:

● tell you something about what you believe your stepchildren think but nothing about what they might really think – unless of course you have had the courage to ask them!

- tell you how little you really do know about their thoughts and feelings.

Now take stock. Use the insight you have developed here. If you have the courage, talk to your stepchildren about these things. At the very least, talk to your partner.

In addition to considering the experiences of stepchildren in the family, we should also look at the kind of relationship which they may find most beneficial with a stepparent. This is our next step in creating the conditions for successful stepparenting.

WHAT DO STEPCHILDREN WANT FROM A STEPPARENT?

There is a very unpalatable truth I must tell you. It will come hard but it is the basis on which you can begin to build a good relationship with your stepchildren. As Brenda Maddox, in *The Half-Parent*, said, 'Stepparents are, in a fundamental sense, unwanted parents'. This is not to say that there can be no love between stepparent and stepchild. Indeed, such a situation is more common than the doom and gloom views about problem stepfamilies convey. Nor are my statements meant to confirm Ann Mitchell's findings, quoted previously, that one child in four with a new parental figure in the home did not like him or her.

Rather, what your stepchild particularly does not want is another mother or father. She or he has one, whether deceased or divorced. Your position, as step, therefore should not attempt to replace the absent parent. Your stepchild does not want a parent substitute. What a stepchild does want, and even need, however is a parent supplement. That is, one who attempts to complement the natural parent. This is how one stepchild expressed it:

'I wanted the attention that my mother gave – because she was my mother – and now she was no longer always there. I wanted my stepmother to make up for the rest. However, I did not want to betray my mother

by sharing the place in my heart she had with my stepmother.'

Time and again I read of the problems stepchildren confront when their stepparents want to step into the shoes of the absent parent as a full replacement. These children are placed in a position of having divided loyalties. Who should they show their support to, their natural parent or their stepparent? In my own research, I talked to one young man, James, whose mother did not have custody but lived nearby. He used to visit her secretly during school lunchtimes. Eventually his stepmother found out and was very hurt and distressed. The very fact that he made his visits in secrecy however suggests how conscious he was of his position of being in the middle, of trying to keep both sides happy. As we heard Emma say earlier, why did her stepmother and stepfather make her feel so guilty for loving her mother and wanting to see her?

ACTIVITY

You as stepchild

Imagine this situation. You are a stepchild standing in the middle of a field. Your stepparent, whom you love very much, is on one side. Your non-custodial parent, whom you also love, is standing on the other side. They are both calling your name. In which direction do you move?

This is an important activity. It will help you to:

● visualise the dilemma of the stepchild;
● perceive that the child can be in a no-win situation.

Remember: You cannot be a parent substitute but you can be a parent supplement.

Let us shift our focus a little now from the stepchild to the stepparent. Our next step is to understand the stepparent's position in the relationship.

STEPPARENTING: YOUR VIEW

This next section looks at the parenting process from your point of view. That is, the stepparent's view. It looks at some of the dilemmas facing the stepparent and considers:

- how they affect you as a stepparent;
- how they affect your stepchild.

PARENT, FRIEND OR NEITHER?

All books on the stepfamily comment on the problems which stepparents have in relation to their stepchildren. Neither parent nor detached friend, they inhabit a shifting territory of responsibilities and expectations. This 'role problem' is central to the difficulties which stepparents face. These difficulties give rise to:

- a sense of uncertainty about the stepparent's proper function;
- a need for some recognition of the stepparent's contribution to the stepchild's upbringing;
- supercharged stepparental emotions.

The stepparent's sense of uncertainty can be seen when we consider the kinds of responsibilities which stepparents have in relation to their stepchildren. Indeed, we have examined many of these in the previous chapters. Stepparents do all the things that natural parents do. They stick plasters on grazed knees and provide the dinner money. They buy the birthday-cake candles and sit up half the night with a sick child, just like any mum or dad.

Yet in essence stepparents are not like any mum or dad. Every so often they are in fact reminded of their ambiguous status. This can come in all kinds of forms: in a fear of disciplining; through a feeling of being an outsider whilst old family histories – before your time – are recounted; quite forcibly when a child shouts 'You're not my mum (or my dad)!'

The access visit is a clear occasion of the stepparent's vulnerability writ large. As a full-time stepparent, you are the main provider of the child's every need, physical and emotional. Yet every so often another parent comes and relieves you of part or all of this. The opposite is true for a part-time stepparent. Here, every so often someone comes and leaves with you the responsibilities of being a provider of physical and emotional care. Is it any wonder you don't quite know where you fit in? One minute you're the parent, the next you feel you have been discarded. Every so often you are reminded that you don't count. Whatever part you play in access visits – either as the recipient of stepchildren as the part-time stepfamily or being relieved of stepchildren in the full-time stepfamily – there is one thing the access visit does for all stepparents. It reminds them of their temporary status.

None of us likes living with ambiguity. It leaves us feeling uncertain about our place in the world. That uncertainty can make us question whether our role as stepparent is worthwhile. If we can be so easily discarded – usually without a backward glance – when the absent parent comes along, what's the point trying to be a decent stepparent. Elizabeth Hodder, in *The Stepparents' Handbook*, suggests that the ensuing resentment can lead to the stepparent withdrawing altogether from a relationship with a stepchild, by becoming distant and cold. It appears to be the only way to cope.

You may also find it helpful to know 'What do stepparents want from their relationship with their stepchildren?' Understanding this is our next step in building successful stepfamilies.

WHAT DO STEPPARENTS WANT?

My answer is that they want to be loved – simple enough at first glance, and something all natural parents take for granted, but not so the hapless stepparent. Love from a stepchild can frequently seem a far-off dream. Too frequently what appears to be absent from the relationship, from the stepparents' point of view, is a sign of emotional commitment from the child. Many stepparents feel that the child gives nothing back in the relationship. This is how one stepmother expressed her feelings:

> 'I dropped my stepson off at work. He walked off without even saying thanks for the lift. I shouted after him "Thanks Jan" [stepmother's name] to make the point. He's the same at home. Never talks to me. Shows me any feeling. I'm the one that bothers about him but he doesn't bother about me. I feel I am the nasty person.'

This stepfather made these comments about his stepdaughter who he considered was seeing life in a rather one-sided way:

> 'What she forgets are all the times I helped her with her homework. How I sat with her for hours to help her through her exams. She was the one who had her bedroom decorated and new carpet first before her sister and brother. It was me who took her to parties and turned out at midnight to bring her back. And it was me who paid for her school trips. Has she forgotten all that?'

Stepparents' feelings that their stepchildren are ungrateful and uncaring throw into relief that all you are is a cook, cleaner, taxi-driver, breadwinner. All the child has to give is love, you say – is that too much to ask? So, the stepparent reasons, if you're not appreciated, let alone loved, what's the point?

This see-sawing of roles is therefore coupled with a see-sawing of emotions. At times you feel wanted and possibly even loved, at others you feel rejected and used. Is it any surprise, therefore, that it is difficult to keep stepfamily life on an even keel for any great length of time? Most books on the stepfamily caution you against taking on the parent replacement role, simply because of the impossibility of this and the problems it brings for stepchildren. Some suggest, somewhat naively, that you should consider yourself a 'special friend'. But even friends get a thank you now and again.

ACTIVITY

Understanding your stepparenting needs

Answer the question: What do you want from your stepchild/ren?

This is an important activity. It will help you to:

- assess your expectations of your stepchild;
- make clear that you have needs too.

In my own research I considered the responses to this seesawing relationship as vitally important to the quality of the stepparent–stepchild relationship. In particular, I think that we have to look at this relationship as one based on mutual give and take. What appears to happen is that, from the stepparent's point of view, the relationship seems to be a one-way traffic. Stepparents, as we have discovered, are already giving a lot to their stepchildren through their hard work and endeavour. They therefore want something in return. This could be gratitude, it could be love, it could be loyalty, it could be to supplant the natural parent in the stepchild's affections. This stepmother's story tells us how her own feelings about her stepdaughter changed when she felt she was getting nothing back from the relationship. The 'something back' she wanted was her stepdaughter's loyalty to her rather than the child's natural mother:

> 'It was all right in the beginning. I tried very hard to be friends with Alice [stepdaughter]. I felt she'd had a

hard time of it and I felt sorry for her. I tried to do it by the book. Be conscientious. Be a friend. Do it properly. Talk to her about what a bad time she'd been through. Buy her new things. Listen to her problems. The problem was, and always has been, her mother. I couldn't stand her mother. Just the thought of her makes my hackles rise. I don't know when it all went wrong. It became like a battle with Alice in the middle. Alice started keeping all these secrets about her mother. Where she was living. What she was doing. You'd know they were lies because things wouldn't add up and you'd catch her out. She became very secretive about her mother and I felt frozen out. I didn't like living in a situation where I didn't know what was going on. It made me uneasy. After that anything Alice said I didn't believe. She'd chosen to side with her mother against me. She'd made it clear where her loyalties lay.'

In my own research I set out case histories of the ways that two different relationships between stepparent and child changed during the course of the study. This was based on the idea that where there is a good relationship between the child and stepparent, the stepparent feels she or he has had some sign of acceptance from the child. In poor relationships, there was evidence that the stepparent felt that she or he had been rejected.

In particular, in the families I studied for over a year, I found that some relationships between stepparent and child improved, some worsened. The question to answer was why?

Take the case of Henry (stepfather) and Ben (stepson, aged four). When I first went to see them Henry felt he had a difficult relationship with Ben. He put this down to the fact that he had little experience of bringing up a son, as he had two daughters from his previous marriage. Boys were therefore an unknown quantity to him. In addition Henry felt Ben was very rejecting of him. Ben would not hold Henry's hand and directed his antagonism at Henry. A book that Henry and Ben's mother read, however, was a turning point. The advice it gave was that you should take children out from time to time individually rather than always going out as a family. This would make them feel special. Accordingly, Henry took Ben to London, during which time Ben held his hand for the first time. This sign of acceptance was a great step forward, as far as Henry was concerned. It culminated in Ben calling Henry 'Dad', something which Henry called 'a major breakthrough'.

In Meg's case, she had experienced what she saw as a series of rejections from her stepdaughter, Sandy. This ranged from being kept on the doorstep if she called on Sandy unexpectedly to being excluded from the birth of her stepgrandchild. Meg felt that she did not count as far as Sandy was concerned and this made their relationship very difficult.

The stark contrasts in the ways these relationships developed highlight how the stepparent looks for signals or signs of the feelings that a stepchild has about them. What stepparents are looking for is an indication that the child is 'on their side'. Without those signs, the stepparent can think all they are is an unthanked workhorse.

ACTIVITY

Are your stepchildren on your side?

Answer the following questions for each stepchild in your family:

Can you identify times when you have felt rejected by your stepchild. List them.

What were your responses to these rejections?

Can you identify times when you have felt accepted by your stepchild? List them.

What were your responses?

This is an important activity. It will help you to:

- assess your relationship with each stepchild;
- assess the ways you react to feeling rejected;
- assess the ways you react to feeling accepted.

It may be that you have different reactions to different children. You may want to consider, therefore, if your responses suggest that one child has become the focus of your feelings of rejection. In consequence the relationship with that child will be poor compared to your relationships with other stepchildren. This is not unusual. There are many cases of stepchildren becoming the scapegoat in a family and so becomes picked on more than other children. Use this activity as a way of understanding why this might be the case in your situation.

Now take stock. Consider the insights you have gained from this exercise and use them to reflect on areas of your relationship with your stepchild which could be improved. You might want to take the advice Henry took and take each child out separately, from time to time. Having tried it, I think it is extremely useful. We behave differently with different children. Even those you like least may surprise you by their affability once you are alone together away from home. Alternatively, you might find that having identified the source of the problem that you are able to overcome it in some way. Allow your finer feelings to diminish the impact of negative experiences on your life!

We have explored in some depth the kind of relationship a stepparent wants from a stepchild. We now need to consider some of our innermost feelings which underpin these expectations.

GETTING IN TOUCH WITH YOUR OWN FEELINGS ABOUT YOUR STEPCHILDREN'S ATTITUDES

Emotions are slippery customers. One moment you can feel good about life, and the next something happens and you are crushed. For many stepparents, a constant problem is the way that your emotions rule your head. Yes, you say, I can understand how I would feel if my parents had split up. The next you are the raging bull, frothing at the mouth at them! We could call this kind of response the 'you versus me' syndrome.

How then do we learn to come to terms with this emotional surcharge? One way is to have a clear idea of the contradictory nature of our feelings and attitudes, that one moment you can have empathy and sympathy for someone and the next only see things from your own side. Take, for example, the findings of the research studies which were set out at the beginning of the chapter. When I first read these I know that my initial feelings were ones of shock at the life experiences of these stepchildren. These initial feelings, however, soon became interwoven with a sense of injustice that these children took no account of all the effort as a stepmother I had made. On the one hand I was concerned that I might have misunderstood all these years the true nature of the children's feelings. On the other I felt anger at their self-centredness. Thus, on the one hand I was concerned about the Other in the relationship – the stepchild. On the other hand, I was concerned about Me.

ACTIVITY

Get in touch with your feelings about stepchildren

- STOP NOW – THINK AND REFLECT
- Go back over the three research studies set out earlier in the chapter. Look at them again.
- How do you feel when you read them?
- List your feelings – anger, sadness, surprise, confirmation of something you've always suspected, and so forth.

When I read the research findings I felt:

This is an important activity. It will help you to:

- begin to see the contradictory nature of your feelings towards stepchildren;
- see the conflicting emotions that can be experienced when you look at situations from different points of view.

Now take stock. Think of a recent situation when you have experienced strong emotions, and reacted accordingly. Consider the following questions:

- Afterwards, did you feel you had been illogical – had your emotions ruled your head?
- Can you pinpoint what had been the turning point or which events had led to your supercharged emotional state?
- You know how you felt. How do you think your stepchild felt?

I do not guarantee that the knowledge you gain from this exercise will solve all the problems which arise when emotions rule your behaviour. What I do suggest is that you use this reflective approach to see if there are patterns to your responses. It may be that even the tiniest insight here will begin to evoke a change to what are often unthinking responses to situations.

Remember: Whilst reciprocity is the ideal, the stepparent feels the reality is one-way traffic.

You should now be in a position to understand how the ambiguous nature of your role as a stepparent can give rise to a mixture of responses and emotions. These emotions can be very hard to live with at times. You should also know how your hopes about the kind of relationship you will have with your stepchildren can place expectations on them to behave towards you in certain kinds of ways. If they do not, that is if you feel they have rejected you, this may lead to you rejecting them. We now turn to another aspect of the stepparenting relationship which, whilst not necessarily deliberate, can leave a child feeling unloved and neglected.

THE UNWANTED STEPCHILD

Were your stepchildren part of the package deal? Did they come as an inevitable addition to loving your partner? Not a very auspicious start from their point of view, is it, to be an unfortunate addendum? Even if you had viewed the prospect of caring for stepchildren with a more positive or welcoming frame of mind, your experiences of courtship will still have been based within the strictures of family life. The research by Burgoyne and Clark in the early 1980s, published as *Making a Go of It*, highlights the way that partners in a stepfamily have very little time to themselves. From day one, their courtship is based around the needs of children and is much more family- and home-centred than is the case for people marrying for the first time. The effect of this is often that courtship and becoming a family – two very distinct stages in a first marriage – become collapsed. You actually never have time to be a couple. Your relationship is most often focused around being a parent – step or otherwise.

For many people, becoming a stepparent is inherently conflictual with wanting to be in a relationship. Without the time to be a couple, partners in a stepfamily strive to find some time alone. This might be at the end of the day when children are in bed, it may be when children visit their absent parent, it may be when you pack them off to their grandparents, as I used to do! In the case of this stepmother, she felt that her needs here were not met, causing resentment and bitterness:

> 'Soon after my husband and I got together we went on holiday with his children. It was terrible. He never thought to put them to bed in the evening until very late. In fact we all went together. Worse than this was that we all shared the same room. There was no getting away from them at all. I couldn't understand why he didn't want to spend some time alone with me. He just never seemed to think.'

I don't think we can underestimate the need to find time to build a relationship with our partner. After all, hopefully you'll still be together long after the stepchildren have left! And we should remember that this is not just important in stepfamily life. The arrival of children in first marriages also means that couples have to find time to maintain a relationship beyond being mum and dad.

My purpose here, however, is not so much to be concerned with your relationship with your partner. Rather, it is the effect that finding space to do this has on your stepchild. Remember Wallerstein and Blakeslee's findings in their research study that many stepchildren feel excluded from the stepfamily? And Emma's comments quoted earlier that she felt a stranger in her own house? Could it be that your understandable need for space and time together contributes to this?

One of the ways to create space is to organise weekends

away without the stepchildren. However, it may be that it is not only the more tangible forms, such as shipping children out of the way, or having a meal in a restaurant without them, which contribute to a stepchild feeling excluded. Indeed, given the legitimacy of these activities, with due sensitivity this may be an area where you should seek little change – indeed may even wish to do more. However, at a more subtle level, there may be ways in which you behave which are less identifiable but more damaging to a stepchild's need to feel they belong. This stepmother talks of a time, early in the relationship, where she could see that her stepson was feeling unwanted:

'It was at a restaurant. My husband – though we weren't married then – sat down. My stepson rushed between us and sat next to his father. You're not sitting next to my Dad, was the look on his face. But I could see that he felt I was taking his rightful place. I know he felt that I was trying to push him out.'

Although this child took his own steps to ensure that he wasn't pushed out, this is not the case for all stepchildren. Brenda Maddox comments on the loneliness of stepchildren she met whilst researching her book. She says that two in particular 'acted like strangers in their own homes', looked unwanted and hung their heads as if apologising for living. There was nothing you could spot as exceptional in the way they were treated; a hesitancy, an awkwardness between stepchild and stepparent. But no words were spoken. No actions were deliberately malevolent.

Do your stepchildren act like strangers in their own home?

ACTIVITY

Anyone missing?

Draw a plan of your living room. It is evening. The television is on.

- Where do you all sit?
- Who sits by whom?
- Is anyone absent from the room? If so, where are they?

This is an important activity. It will help you to:

- look at patterns of family relationships;
- know whether stepchildren absent themselves from this family activity.

Now take stock. Look at your plan and answer the following questions:

- Would you say that the seating position on your plan indicates close and distant relationships in your family?
- Look at your position in relation to your partner? Would you say that this could make children feel excluded?
- Does a child spend a lot of time alone, in their bedroom? This may reflect their age – my teenage stepson spends a lot of his time in his room whereas when he was younger he didn't. However, a child's response to feeling unwanted could be to absent themselves. A key question to ask is 'How do you feel about their absence?' If you're pleased, could it indicate that this is the case?

There is no point my preaching at you to change your behaviour if your results from this activity make you suspect that a stepchild feels uncared for. Our responses to our stepchildren are far more deeply embedded within complex thoughts and attitudes than we could possibly tap through this book. Nevertheless, you may wish to create more physical space for stepchildren to sit by a loved parent, or to help them feel loved by choosing to sit by – and even cuddle – them.

It may be that you cannot take on this responsibility yourself because you dislike your stepchild. It may help, therefore, for you to know that the parental figure is not the only source from which a child can gain love and respect. Let yourself off the hook a little, if it cannot be you who is this source. Stepchildren have their natural parents and grand-parents. They may even now have stepgrandparents. They also have aunts and uncles. So whilst you cannot be the font of all love for a stepchild, it may be that someone within the family is. To assuage some of your undoubted guilt, you may take the responsibility to ensure that someone within the extended family is providing this much needed care. Your role here could be, say, to make any necessary arrangements. This way you have made your contribution to a child's well-being, not directly in this case, but through acting as a responsible adult.

Remember: The stepparent is not the child's only source of love and attention.

THE WICKED STEPCHILD

We have considered at length the problems of being seen as a wicked stepmother. Yet as I pointed out in Chapter One many stepparents think that a stepchild is wicked. Try this quiz to find out if you are one!

ACTIVITY

Have you got a wicked stepchild?

Have you ever said any of the following?

	YES	NO
1 He's just like his father		
2 She's just like her mother		
3 You can't tell by his face that he's lying		
4 You can't tell by her face that she's lying		
5 My stepchild is always keeping secrets		
6 You can never be sure what your stepchild is thinking		
7 You can guess what she's been saying about me		
8 You can guess what he's been saying about me		

SCORE:
- Count how many 'yes' answers you have.
- Nil. Either you are lying or you are a paragon of virtue.
- 1–8 You need to read on to understand why you say these things!

All of the statements in the last exercise have been made to me by stepparents about their stepchildren. But more importantly than that, they were said about stepchildren with whom they were experiencing difficulties and who they even hated. Hating a stepchild is not an uncommon experience. Brenda Maddox describes very graphically in her book the feelings of some stepparents towards their stepchildren – a feeling of physical revulsion at the sight of a stepchild, being glad when they are out of sight and consequently out of mind. The knowledge that you are not alone in feeling this way can be quite liberating. It means that you are not necessarily the uniquely evil person you thought you were.

Nevertheless, this does not answer the question of why you might have these feelings. One response could be that the child is indeed unlovable. First of all, perhaps we shouldn't always be too ready to see the child as a poor trapped innocent with no will of their own. Anyone who has experienced the temper tantrum of a toddler or the slamming doors of a teenager will know that children can be incredibly wilful if they so desire. Children are not always victims therefore. They can also sometimes effect the change they desire. Some years ago, during a radio phone-in programme on the stepfamily, one teenage girl rang in to say that she had not liked any of her mother's boyfriends. She had gone to various lengths to ensure successfully that they did not stay around for long. This behaviour was not unconscious or accidental. It was planned and deceitful.

However, we should not forget that, as a group, children in our society are relatively powerless. They might be able to kick up a stink in the family once in a while; they may even, as in the case above, ensure potential stepfathers do not become actual ones. They are, however, still dependent on the adults who care for them to provide stability, emotional security and even a roof over their heads.

Elizabeth Hodder, in *The Stepparents' Handbook*, talks about the problems of disliking your stepchild as resulting in 'a chain of destructive behaviour making it impossible for you to consider any form of relationship with the stepchildren'. She says that the guilt one feels about not loving a stepchild or stepchildren leads the stepmother to turn this into excuses that the child is actually unlovable. Hating your stepchildren is not, in fact, uniquely a stepmother problem. Stepfathers I have spoken to have similar feelings. One stepfather in my own research study told me how he found the reality of living with his stepchildren very distressing. He commented that he felt that their 'personal habits' were distasteful and 'over-powering'.

Is Elizabeth Hodder right in saying that stepparents turn this around into ways which make their feelings acceptable? That stepparents blame the stepchild for their own unlova-bility. Let's consider this a little by looking at what underpins the statements which formed the quiz at the beginning of this section.

As I've said, these statements have been made to me by very many stepparents. In my own research study I used them as one way of understanding a little about how relation-ships between stepparent and stepchild develop. What appeared to be happening was that the stepparent felt rejected by a stepchild or felt the stepchild was acting against them. They then began to construct a list of the stepchild's behaviours which supported this view that the stepchild was indeed working against them. Take, for example, the state-ment 'You can guess what she/he has said about me.' Here the stepparent believes that the stepchild tells stories about them which makes the stepparent appear wicked and the stepchild appear a modern-day Cinderella or Cinderfella. Listen to this stepparent's account:

'I don't know what it is but when her friends come round I feel as though they think I'm really nasty. She's probably told them all about me and they think it's true that she's got a real wicked stepmother. They don't say anything. In fact that could be the problem. They're never friendly. They treat me as if I've upset them in some way. There's just this atmosphere. I'm sure she's

told all sorts of stories about me to get them to feel sorry for her.'

With the statement 'He's just like his father' or 'She's just like her mother', the stepparent sees the way that a child acts as replicating the non-custodial parent's behaviour. There may be a lot of bad feeling towards that parent (see Chapter Five for discussion of this). The child's behaviour patterns are seen to be similar to those the stepparent has found so intolerable in the non-custodial parent. For example, one stepmother told me that her stepdaughter was going to turn out just like her mother, in that she wouldn't be able to sustain a relationship with a man for any length of time. 'She'll end up being a slut just the same as her mother,' she said.

Lying is another trait that stepchildren are supposed to exhibit. Whether they do in reality is a hard question to answer, although I think all children must lie from time to time. However, when stepparents talk about stepchildren as liars they are actually saying that they can't trust them. The statement 'You can't tell by their face that they're lying' speaks of the stepparents' own lack of knowledge of a child's normal behavioural responses. It is the very opposite of what many natural parents say about their children: 'I can always tell when he's lying by the look on his face.' That statement is built on the knowledge of a child from babyhood, something a stepparent doesn't have. Similarly, statements such as 'You can never be sure' and 'They're always keeping secrets' also display the stepparents' fears and insecurity.

What is interesting about these statements is the way that they are often built on the flimsiest of evidence. On what stepparents will describe as 'Just a feeling'. This evidence then becomes catalogued as a list of examples of the stepchild's misdemeanours. Unfortunately, there is almost no way back from this point. The child becomes the wicked one in the family – some would call the scapegoat. All intense feelings are focused on this child and they are locked into a self-fulfilling prophecy. Once the child is labelled as wicked everything he or she does is seen to be wicked.

What can we do about this, if indeed Elizabeth Hodder is right that we have started a 'chain of destructive behaviour'? I hope the final activity in this chapter will help you.

ACTIVITY

What stories can you tell about your stepchild?

Think of one of the comments in the quiz above that you have said about a stepchild.

- Can you recount a series of incidents which support this view of your stepchild?
- Do you have tangible evidence for your attitude or is it just a feeling?

This is an important activity. It will help you to:

- identify a chain of incidents which support your view;
- suggest that there might be an element of doubt to your view.

Now take stock. Answer these questions:

- Do you feel this stepchild dislikes you?
- Do you feel this stepchild is ungrateful about all you have done in the family?

If you have answered Yes to either of these questions, is there any chance that this is the reason why you now have bad feelings about a stepchild? That you felt rejected, and so have rejected them?

If your answers are No it may be that you have still projected your guilt about not loving a child into making them unlovable. Making them unlovable is easy when you have a catalogue of their misdemeanours. Search your conscience. Could you be doing this?

REVIEW

The key messages of this chapter are:

- there are two sides to the stepparent–stepchild relationship;
- try to understand your stepchild's view point;
- the stepparent's role has inbuilt tensions. Your experiences replicate these tensions;
- stepchildren can be seen by stepparents to be just as wicked as the stepchildren view their stepmothers.

Remember: As much as we'd like, none of us is the perfect stepparent. In fact most of us simply progress from crisis to crisis and cope as best we can as we go. Keep on coping.

5

JUST A SECOND

Secondhand rose, second best, china shop 'seconds' – we all know that 'second time around' has that slightly tainted feel to it. It is full of all the negative stereotypes that we discussed in Chapter One about the stepfamily. But this time it's more personal. Being a second wife or husband smacks uncomfortably of being a second choice. As Glynnis Walker, in her book *Second Wife, Second Best?*, comments so well, all wives are not created equal. Can we say the same about second husbands?

There certainly is truth in the comment that the second spouse has to live in the shadow of the first. If it weren't enough to find oneself parenting their children, you can also find yourself living in their old house, feeling that they control all your weekends and holidays, having to deal with their animosity. Living in someone else's shadow may lead you to think you have got to become a super-wife or super-husband just to stay competing in the game. And competition it certainly can feel.

As a second spouse, your experience of marriage will in many, many ways be different to the experience of those in first marriages. You are likely to be poorer for a start. The costs of divorce can resonate through the post-divorce years and you may find you never get yourself back into the position you might have been in had this been a first marriage. The major decisions in your life about where you live and how many children you have will also be affected by the fact that this relationship is 'second time around'. Your housing may be tied to the results of divorce settlements. The number of children you have, or whether indeed you have any at all, will be affected by the existence of your step-children.

If this were not enough, the ex-partner will always be someone in your life. As a stepfamily, your link to them will be reinforced through your stepchildren. Your step-children may look like them and so at times you may feel you are actually living with their absent parent. Your step-children will be in contact with them, regularly or irregularly. At birthdays and Christmas, much as you dislike it, there will be some reminder of their existence.

This chapter is about these unique features of a second marriage. It considers the way that a second marriage requires you to make different decisions and gives you different options from a first marriage. These relate to:

- ensuring you have a home not a house;
- making decisions about more children;
- dealing with the ex in your life – whether divorced or deceased.

The chapter takes you through each of these issues, guiding you through some of the processes that affect your decision-making and encouraging you to take a fresh look at some of the most difficult areas of your life. Fundamentally, this chapter is about how to manage your position as a 'second' rather than letting it manage you.

Remember: The distinctive problems of second marriage can require distinctive solutions.

YOUR HOUSE, MY HOUSE, OUR HOUSE

One of the common problems facing stepfamilies is the fact that they often start out in a house that was one of the partner's marital home. One person moves into the house that their new partner shared with his or her previous partner. Whilst there is no doubt that this can be convenient, it does bring its own penalties. These are:

- the feelings of your stepchildren;
- the problem of creating your own identity in your new surroundings.

The problem you confront is how you achieve making this house into your home without jeopardising your relationship with your stepchildren. As you will have seen, in Chapter Four, Emma was particularly concerned at the way her stepmother changed her surroundings and changed the way her family had always celebrated Christmas. You need to turn your living quarters into a place where you can feel relaxed and comfortable, and at the same time you have to try to minimise the extent to which your stepchildren may think that their feelings are being ignored. It appears that, often, these two needs are working in opposition.

The need to create a sense of identity in the place where you live is perfectly natural. When a couple or a family buy or move into a house, what is the first thing that they do? They put their own furnishings in, they might decorate, they might plant new plants in the garden. As I write, I am watching my neighbour who bought the house next door to me just a few weeks ago. He is digging up the lawn that has been at the side of the house for the past six years and is replacing it with a flower bed. A new garden shed has arrived as well. Perhaps my new neighbour is a keen gardener. It certainly seems to me that he is keen to change things, to stamp his own identity on the property and to make it feel like 'his' home. We can see this kind of thing every day.

From the child's point of view, of course, things are rather different. Children like stability. They don't like change. Take my daughter, aged six, as an example. Our house is currently blighted by a compulsory purchase order for one of the country's first toll roads. We consequently often talk about moving. We are not looking forward to the motorway running through our garden. Our daughter is devastated and will hear nothing of us moving house. She becomes upset if we look at other houses and insists she does not want to live anywhere else.

It is not only about the big issues of moving house that children show their attachment to material things. This was very sensitively expressed to me by the parents of a friend of my stepson. This family had decided, a few years ago, to move to Australia. They sold their house and almost all their belongings. Their mother told me that they would, of course, be taking their lounge suite and a few other items of furniture so that when they arrived in their new house in Australia 'there would still be something familiar for the children'. This mother had understood that her children, while experiencing change in their lives, needed continuity. This continuity would enhance their sense of stability.

We have, therefore, a situation where the stepparent needs to feel at home in their new surroundings but where the stepchild does not need to be threatened by the way that the stepparent fulfils this need. Changing and replacing can certainly lead to a threatening situation from the child's point of view. From the stepparent's it is a necessary step to eliminate the ghost of the previous partner.

This is the additional burden that the incoming stepparent has to bear. Not only do they want, in a very natural and everyday sense, to establish their personal identity in their living-space, but the living-space they are about to inhabit is also the one that was inhabited by their partner's previous partner. The cooker you cook on will be the same as she or he cooked on. The bed you sleep in will be the same as she or he shared with your partner. The sun lounger you get out of the garden shed is likely to be the one she or he bought only last year. Moving into someone else's house, as a new partner, means not only imposing yourself on your surroundings. It means eradicating the ghost of the previous partner.

Again, this presents problems for stepchildren. This 'ghost' is their parent. The last thing they want is that parent eradicated. So once more, you have an opposition of needs. Yours against theirs. You need, for your sanity, to get rid of your partner's ex. They need, for their sanity, to keep that parent as close as possible. Stalemate.

What do you do? The answer is to go ...

---

very very very very very very very very very very very
very very very very very very very very very very very
very very very very very very very very very very very
very very very very very very very very very very very
very very very very very very very very very very very
very very very very very very very very very very very
very very very very very very very very SLOWLY!!!

Yes, take it easy! Don't rush in like a bull in a china shop sweeping out that ghastly carpet and lounge suite, even if they are beyond the pale. If you do, it is likely your stepchildren will show an attachment to them that astounds their parent, let alone you. To them you are throwing out their absent parent.

How are you to proceed therefore? I have listed some tips to help you establish your identity in your new domain.

MAKING 'THEIR' HOUSE FEEL LIKE 'YOUR' HOME AS WELL

TWELVE TIPS

---

1 **Don't change anything at all.** To your stepchildren you are the invader. You are entering their personal space. To your partner, you are an invited invader! When you first move in don't change anything at all. You have enough to do in establishing relationships with your partner and stepchildren without trying to change their accommodation. Indeed, from their point of view they may not see that

there is any need for any change. More than likely, they like it just as it is.

2 **Don't change everything all at once.** Much as you would like to, try to resist stripping off the old wallpaper, repainting the front door and moving the furniture around in the first few weeks. Do these jobs as and when they are necessary.

3 **Think of adding rather than taking away.** When you first move into someone else's house your instinct is to get rid of items that you do not like or those that represent the natural parent. Refrain from doing this, at least in the early days. It is more positive to think of adding to what is already there rather than taking away. This way you can leave things much as they are but also contribute items that help you feel that you live there too. These items might be small things, like a vase or crockery. They might be large things, like an extension or conservatory. Indeed, if you are fortunate enough to be able to afford it, building on to a house will give you the space to call your own and the opportunity to furnish and decorate from scratch. You will have added to their home and satisfied your most immediate needs without jeopardising your step-children's needs for familiarity and continuity.

4 **Create some place in the house you can call your own.** Do not underestimate how important it is to have some part of your house that you can call your own. Houses are full of communal space yet we still have a need to go somewhere, sometimes, where we can be alone or to display our most precious possessions. Teenagers are very good at this when they turn their bedrooms almost into bedsits. Take a tip from them – your bedroom might be a good place. Put a television up there. Even a garden shed

which you can grandly call the summer house or 'Mary's Extension' will give you a place where you can get away from your stepfamily once in a while. Ensure electricity is connected and you can hang up curtains at the windows, put in an old chair, get a book, play some music, watch some soaps on TV and relax, in *your* place.

5 **Consult your stepchildren and your partner.** Whilst you are sorting through cupboards and drawers in your zeal to establish some order in your new home, remember to ask your partner and stepchildren if there is anything they want to keep. Whilst it all may look like years of accumulated rubbish to you, to them you could be about to throw away objects to which they have attached some of their most cherished memories.

6 **Negotiate.** If you are bringing two homes together, it may be you have to trade with your partner if you have both got the same items of furniture. Don't forget partners can have an emotional attachment to objects in just the same way as stepchildren. Again, consult the stepchildren – they may even prefer some of your furniture to their own. Their involvement will also give them a chance to have a sense of ownership about the decisions that are made.

7 **Do not touch anything in your stepchildren's bedrooms without their express agreement and involvement.** A child's bedroom is their personal space littered as it might be with toys, comics, stale drinks and sweet papers. This is a place where you should tread very carefully or tread not at all.

8 **When combining two families with two sets of children try to ensure they have a bedroom each.** It can be difficult when families come together to find

enough space for all your belongings let alone be sure you have enough bedroom space for your children. Try, if at all possible, to allow all children to have their own room. If this is not possible, think of splitting the room with some kind of partition or curtain or try to arrange the furniture so that each child has a sense of their own private space. Children need privacy just as much as adults.

9 **Respect children's wishes about sharing.** If space is at a premium and children have to, ask your children with whom they would like to share. Respect their wishes and don't try to force the issue. Allow children to know that this is not a lifetime commitment. If they find they don't get on, or after a time would prefer to share with another sibling or stepsibling, this should be built into the agreement from the beginning. This might save some heartbreak when John has decided that it looks like more fun to share with James and Harry is wondering what he has done to deserve being deserted. In the event of children arguing and falling out, you have also given everyone permission to move around without this becoming too big an issue.

10 **Don't forget the needs of visiting stepchildren.** Here the situation could be reversed, when children come to visit what is, to them, not your house alone but their new parent's house as well. Although research suggests that children are actually very adaptable at seeing the place where their parent lives as their home too, don't make a visiting stepchild feel like a stranger or a visitor. They will appreciate some sign of continuity and still need a sense of belonging. Try to have a place which is just for them and allow them to leave some of their own belongings with you permanently. Ensure they at

least have their own proper bed, not a put-me-up, which is permanently in a bedroom if you have not got the space to let them have a room of their own. There is nothing more likely to make a child feel like a visitor as having to make up a bed for them on the sofa or on the floor of one of the other children's bedrooms every time they visit.

11 **Moving house: the stepparent's view.** Ultimately moving house may prove to be the most satisfactory solution from the stepparent's viewpoint. This is because you will probably never completely eradicate the 'ghost' of living in someone else's house until you do. I know this was my own feeling and the day we moved from my partner's previous marital home was the one when I began to feel I really had got a place where I belonged. However, you should be careful of the timing of this as moving house, like others of life's major events, can be very stressful. You will already have been through some stressful situations in your recent past. You have to ask yourself whether you can cope with another one or whether it is better to wait. You will also need to consider how moving house may affect your financial position. Buying a bigger house to suit your growing stepfamily's needs may be ideal, but does it mean taking on a bigger mortgage just when things are tight?

12 **Moving house: the stepchild's view.** From the stepchild's viewpoint, moving house may not seem the great idea you think it is. A child may see the prospect of moving as the final cutting of old ties and one they strongly do not want to make. They will have been through the same series of stressful events as the adults in their lives. Can they take another? Children will also naturally worry a great deal about losing touch with friends

in the neighbourhood as well as whether moving house means they also have to leave the hamster behind. You will need to think through very carefully how moving house will affect (1) access arrangements – will the child's absent parent find it more difficult to see the child?; (2) schooling – can the child cope with a change of school? Are they at a stage where it would be foolish to change? You would be unwise to move a child in the years preceding examinations; (3) the extended family – never underestimate the importance of a child's ties to their grandparents, cousins, aunts and uncles. Will your stepchildren still be able to see them easily? My stepchildren were 'lucky' in the sense that my instinct was to move house as soon as we became a stepfamily. Continuing problems over my partner's divorce and the housing market prevented this for four years. In retrospect, whilst this was not very good for me, for them it was probably for the best. It gave them some breathing space to get to know me in their own territory. Sometimes it seems external circumstances do have a way of working out for the best.

These tips are designed to help you think through some of the issues when two families find themselves living together and both need to feel they are living in their home not someone else's house. Deborah Fowler, in her book *Loving Other People's Children*, reminds the stepparent who moves into a former marital home that they are treading on eggshells. I hope these tips will stop you from crushing those eggshells to powder!

Remember: We all need to feel 'at home' in a house. Create space for yourself and your stepfamily.

THE 'OUR' CHILD

Having an 'our' child has been, for me, the best decision I ever made in my life and one I have never regretted for one single moment. I adore my daughter, live for her, breathe for her. She has made my stepfamily complete and fulfilled within me many deep emotional needs. I believe she has also made us into a family in a very real sense. To her, my stepchildren are her brother and sister fully and entirely. There are no halves. She loves them both without any reservation. They are her family. Have I just been lucky?

The longing for a child can be an immense desire for many people. Having a child can be a way of fulfilling our own needs. It can change a couple into a family. It can be a way of committing ourselves to someone else. Having a child in a stepfamily, however, is rather a different enterprise from having a child in a first family.

In a first family, there is often an assumption that you will have children. Your mother asks you when you are going to make her a grandmother. Your in-laws talk endlessly about their child-rearing days in the evident hope that many of their happy memories will be rekindled with grandchildren. Mostly, therefore, decisions about having a child are framed around the questions 'When?' 'How many?' and 'How far apart?' Your thinking on this issue will be determined by whether you should have children early in your relationship or wait until you have established yourself in your home. You may think you should wait until you have been able to afford all the essentials and luxuries you want or have got to a certain stage in your career before embarking on parenthood. Alternatively, you may be of the view that children benefit most from having young parents and waiting longer only means that you will be older and possibly less adaptable when children arrive.

Is it better to have your children close together or is it better to have a gap so that you can give each child some individual attention without the inevitable competition of a closely aged sibling? Should you have one, two, three or four? Whatever you decide, this is normally the process first families go through.

However, things are a little different in the stepfamily. Stepfamilies already have children. The questions of 'When?' 'How many?' and 'How far apart?' have already been decided, to some extent. For the stepfamily the question really becomes 'Should we?' The answer depends on so many factors. We shall consider these as:

- no doubts: we want a child;
- overcoming problems: stepchildren;
- 'not allowed' to have children;
- not for us.

No Doubts: We Want a Child

The desire to have a child in a stepfamily sometimes faces overwhelming odds. Most couples in first marriages certainly do not plan for divorce or remarriage. Consequently, decisions are not usually made with these events in mind. For example, decisions over future fertility are made in the here and now. Once you have had your 2.3 children you may decide that enough is enough. One partner may in consequence be sterilised. However, in the event of a remarriage, the desire for children may become rekindled. Yet how could you anticipate it? One couple in my own research study certainly found themselves in this situation. The husband had had a vasectomy some years previously. His wife had since died and he remarried a much younger woman. She already had two children but had always seen herself as having at least four. They decided that they would try to have some more children. This required the husband to have a reversal operation and fertility treatment. It entailed a lot of concern and worry. Happily, their endeavours were rewarded. The wife became pregnant and has since had two more children.

There are certainly many positive factors associated with having an 'our' child:

- such a child can be a sign that this new relationship is for keeps. Having a baby is a commitment that you intend to stay together. This may help stepchildren feel more secure in their relationship with you. It may make them feel that you are not going to disappear out of their lives in the very near future;
- a child is a way of uniting both sides of the family. The 'our' child is the link between two separate families and so can give you all a bond;
- a child can become a focus of love for stepchildren. The 'our' child comes into the world untainted with the memories of previous relationships. The stepchild and the 'our' child can represent a chance for both to create their own unique and loving relationship.

OVERCOMING PROBLEMS: STEPCHILDREN

Although partners may agree that they want to have another child, we should remember that they are not the only ones who have feelings about more children in the household. Children and stepchildren can also forcefully show their feelings. They may see any further children as reducing the amount of love there is to go round. They may, with a sense of realism, see their inheritance reducing as it has to be shared amongst more offspring. They may not like the idea because of the clear evidence that more children means their parents are still sexually active. As all research indicates, children find this aspect of their parent's life the most difficult to accept. The idea of acknowledging their parents' sexual life can be quite repugnant to a child, particularly an adolescent one who has their own sexuality to think through.

The stepmother I have just mentioned, whose partner underwent a vasectomy reversal, met quite a lot of initial hostility from her stepchildren at the idea of acquiring a half-sibling. They told their stepmother that they were against the whole thing. However, if she went ahead she must have girls as they were not used to boys in their house! Quite a tall order but she managed to pull it off!

In addition, we know only too well that all mother and baby books warn you of the incipient jealousies that having a child can create. Your spouse will feel pushed out and jealous. Your children similarly. Will having a child mean you neglect your stepchildren? One stepmother I know considered that having her own child was the turning point, for the worse, in her relationship with her stepson. She had been his stepmother since he was four and described their relationship as wonderful. She said they were close and loved each other very much. They went everywhere and shared everything together. She had her child when her stepson was aged 11. She said her stepson was thrilled and she has pictures of him with his half-sister cradling and cuddling her as a baby. Yet since that time, her relationship with her stepson had gone sadly wrong. Now they hardly speak and she considers he is no more than a lodger in her house. Yet she says:

'If I am honest with myself it went wrong when Rebecca was born. I pushed him out. All I wanted was my daughter. I pushed everyone out.'

This is certainly a sad outcome of such a happy and eagerly anticipated event and one we can learn much from. Whilst we have focused in Chapter Four on the dangers of feeling rejected by a stepchild, we should of course also consider that there are similar dangers that a stepchild may feel rejected by us.

The need to take account of stepchildren's feelings is certainly important when making decisions of this kind and this is another problem that you may have to overcome. Stepchildren will have to live with the repercussions of a new baby just as you will. For example:

- consider the age gaps between children. Children have different needs at different times. Will you find yourself in an impossible situation when the demands of babyhood clash with the demands of adolescence?
- time. Babies mean less time all round. This means less time

for other children. Your present children need you now. Have you got enough time for them and another one?

- love. Your stepchildren will need to be convinced that you will continue to love them after the new baby has arrived.

Remember: Your current children, step or otherwise, need you just as much as a new baby will.

'NOT ALLOWED' TO HAVE CHILDREN

Whilst some couples may agree on remarriage that they want more children, in some stepfamilies this is not the case. In particular, one partner may be sure that this is not for them. The other may be sure that it is. This can certainly be a problem when one of you has not had children previously, although it is not exclusive to that state. I have met many stepparents who have children from previous marriages and continue to want to seal their new relationship with another baby. The need for a child is also not exclusively female. Many men want a child just as much as women. Indeed, Brenda Maddox, in *The Half-Parent*, comments that a stepparent who longs for a child has much frustration to bear. This situation is just as hard for men as it is for women.

I have often heard women say to me, 'I am not allowed to have a child.' What do they mean by this statement? My understanding is that they are saying loudly and clearly, 'I want children. My partner does not. He is preventing me from having them.' One stepmother I know is married to a man whose children are now in their late teens and beginning to leave home. He is adamant that his days of nappy-changing and being tied to the needs of a child are over. He is looking forward to the loosening of responsibilities and is quite sure he does not want to be tied down in this way again. This has been his position since the early days of the relationship, though I guess that this stepmother has always nurtured a secret hope that he will change his mind. Will he? Even if he does, will he feel it was under duress? These are certainly issues to be considered.

However, when stepmothers say 'I am not allowed to have children' they are also questioning the basis of their relationship with their partner. 'I'm not allowed but she was' is the way this questioning goes, 'she' being the partner's ex. Why, the stepmother asks herself, should I be expected to look after 'their' children when I'm not allowed to have any of my own? Indeed, on the face of it this is certainly unjust. More than this, however, the danger is that the stepmother can begin to think that her stepchildren have 'stolen her fertility'. This is a phrase that Brenda Maddox uses in *The Half-Parent*. She is referring to the fact that many stepmothers seem to have trouble in becoming pregnant. The existence of stepchildren, in her experience, can create a psychological block. The women who say 'I'm not allowed' see themselves being denied the chance even to try. For them, their fertility has truly been stolen.

We may hope that time will change our partner's views. We can even misread all the signs. They've already got children so there won't be any problems about more, you reason to yourself. Indeed, the fact that your partner already had children may be one of the things that attracted you to them in the first place. If you admired the way they parented their own children, you may have thought these were qualities you would like to see in the father or mother of your own. An adult with children can also seem a safer bet than one who is single. You may have perceived them as more settled down and so more willing to be settled down than a single person. How correct your judgements were you will only find out by talking about this with your partner. It appears, however, that if the man or woman in your life has always told you that they don't want any more children, believe them. It is doubtful they will happily change their mind. What you have to ask yourself is, can you live with that?

The desire to have a child can also be experienced quite differently by women and men. In particular, women have to take account of their biological clock whilst men do not. Men can play around with the idea of having a child almost indefinitely as many of the sixty-year-old fathers illustrate. Women can't. By the time they reach their thirties they are already seen as 'old' mothers by the medical profession. By their late thirties time is certainly running out. This in itself can create pressures and delusion in a stepfamily. As a woman in your twenties you may feel that having children is not that important. Moreover, your experience of step-children could be enough to have put you off the thought of motherhood for life! Nevertheless, as you reach your early to mid-thirties a nagging begins. I wonder if I really do want children after all? you ask yourself.

It may help to think through how important this issue is for you. Having and not having children can equally be a source of regret. Don't make any decision you may regret. The following activity is very simple. It asks you to use your imagination and search your soul. It may not give you an absolute solution. It will point you in the right direction though.

ACTIVITY

WHEN I'M 65

Imagine:

You are 65 and did not have children in this relation-ship. How do you feel?

This is an important activity. It will help you:

- to think about the importance of an 'our' child in your current relationship;
- if you are currently childless, to think about the importance to you individually of having a child.

For some stepparents, there is no need to think about whether or not to have an 'our' child. They are quite sure that more children are not for them. This is the final part in considering the issues of the 'our' child.

Not For Us!

In their research into the stepfamily, Jackie Burgoyne and David Clarke identified a group of stepparents as 'looking forward to the departure of their children'. These are often couples who have teenage children and who are waiting for these children to leave so that they can have a relationship without the interruptions and problems that children bring. They can become a couple and no longer a family!

Couples who are sure that they do not want any more children have decided that the disadvantages outweigh the advantages. The problems of children should certainly not be discounted in your decision-making. They are truly real in their consequences. A new baby has never made a shaky relationship into a secure one. It is more likely to work in reverse and add pressures that can make even the most stable couples into unstable ones. These are the problems you might like to consider:

- Babies mean broken nights, teething, tiredness and nappies. Can you put up with it, especially if it's second time around?
- The mother's age. Settling into a new stepfamily, going through divorce or widowhood, have all added time. This can mean that many stepmothers who want to become mothers are older women. It is important to consider the health implications of age, especially with regard to the mother's own health needs and the baby's. You will need to think about the risks of having a disabled child and take professional medical advice about your own health as well.
- Cost. There is no doubt that children cost money. Can you afford another child? It may be particularly difficult if your

income is already seriously diminished through paying maintenance for children of another relationship. In addition to the direct costs of children, a new baby will make other financial demands. Is your car big enough to carry you all, plus a new baby? Have you got enough space in your house? Will having another child reduce the amount you have to spend on other children in a serious way?

- Work. If you are both already in paid work, will having a baby mean one of you will have to give this up? Can you afford the loss of income? It may be advisable to check your situation with regard to maternity benefits and maternity leave. The rules vary according to length of service and number of hours worked per week. If you are planning to become or already are a working mother can you manage this and the demands of children? Use the organisations and books listed on pages 213–26 if you need further advice on these issues. Finally, if you are planning to give up work, how will you feel about this? Although many women are extremely fulfilled bringing up their young children, others find it isolating and can become depressed. You may want to think about how giving up paid work can affect your future career and work prospects. There are few women, today, who can afford to give up work for good once children arrive. Some planning here will pay dividends later.

- Is this relationship for keeps? Having a baby is not something that should be undertaken lightly. You will need to think about how a baby will affect all aspects of your relationships in your family. What would your situation be in the event of a separation and divorce?

- Can you accept being tied down? Children have a unique way of tying you down. Gone is the spontaneity of popping out to the shops and going to the pub. Feed and sleep times will dominate your day. You may feel that you are already tied down by children as it is, and a baby will make little difference. A baby will, however, extend this period.

- A baby may add problems rather than solve them. You may already be experiencing problems in your relationships with children and stepchildren. You will need to consider carefully if another child could make these worse. It may be worth thinking of waiting for a while until current problems have passed, if this is the case.

If you really want a baby, no matter how much the disadvantages outweigh the advantages you are likely to go ahead. On a positive note, it does appear that the 'our' child has a markedly beneficial effect on most stepfamilies and this is something we can note with pride. It indicates how much parents and children work together to make their family life successful. However, this next activity will help you to sort through some of the issues you will need to consider when making your decision and is designed to help you formulate your own list of advantages and disadvantages.

ACTIVITY

THE 'OUR' BABY

Some questions to help you think about this:

1 Are both I and my partner in total agreement about this issue?
2 How do the children/stepchildren feel?
3 What are the cost implications? Can we afford it?
4 How do I feel about being tied down by a baby?
5 Is this the right time?

This is an important activity. It will help you to:

- check you have taken the feelings of your stepfamily into account;
- have a clear idea of the impact another child will make in your life.

Remember: Children are like dogs. You have them for life.

THE WICKED EX-WIFE

Despite popular opinion, evidence from the stepfamily suggests that the battle of the sexes is not between women and men. It is between women and women. The prize? A man. The title of Shirley Eskapa's book *Woman versus Woman* portrays this situation extremely well. Her book is about the eternal triangle, the wife, the mistress, the husband. Her thesis? That marriages can survive an affair, that wives are very adept at sabotaging the other woman. Perhaps the second wife has much to learn from the first here about reversing the situation!

Accounts of remarriages are filled with similar tales of hatred, jealousy, rivalry and tactical planning. The ex-wife becomes 'she most hated', the real 'she-devil' in the relationship. This is how one stepmother described her partner's first wife:

> 'She's everything conniving, back stabbing, devious, self-centred, and self-motivated. I wouldn't trust her. She's unreliable as far as the children are concerned. Having her around there's this part of you that creates an insecurity in you. Just knowing she's there and that brings about a defensive feeling. I basically look very much side ways at her. She's one big actress. Trying to look good to her parents. She tries to look good as far as the kids are concerned if her parents are about. Otherwise she doesn't bother. We call her the dragon lady. Apparently she suffers from haemorrhoids. We just call her a pain in the arse. If we saw her in the street we'd cross to the other side.'

If a current partner does not totally dislike their predecessor, it is clear that neither would she describe her as a friend or someone she would voluntarily spend her time with. This is what one stepmother said to me about her partner's ex:

> 'We've always got on okay but I wouldn't say she was my kind of person. She's not someone I would choose to spend time with.'

This leaves us to ask what is so wrong with the ex-wife that it can lead to such a range of feelings, stretching from hatred to cool disdain? We shall consider the way that attitudes towards a previous partner are built up by discussing:

- what is so wicked about the ex?
- how does the ex get to be seen as wicked in the first place?

WHAT IS SO WICKED ABOUT THE EX?

All the evidence suggests that women judge other women according to two main criteria – how good they are at mothering and how good they are at being a wife. It would seem that most ex-partners fall short on both counts.

When it comes to mothering, many stepmothers describe how poor their predecessor was in this respect. She will often be described as a pretty terrible mother and I have heard (and have told them myself!) many tales of neglect and selfishness. This stepmother describes her stepson's mother's interest in him as based purely on her own selfish needs:

> 'She's only interested in him now because he's useful. He will be able to help her with the odd jobs around the house.'

This stepmother describes how neglectful the mother can be in the care of her children's safety:

> 'She had the children for the weekend. They told us that they'd gone out for some chips from the chippy down the road. When we asked if their mother was with them they said she wasn't. We were horrified. What sort of mother is she to let her children cross a busy main road on their own at night?'

The following stepmother echoes what many women say when a mother decides to take the ultimate unmotherly step and leave her children behind when she separates from her partner:

'What I can never understand is how any woman could leave her kids. What sort of mother is she?'

Women also judge other women on the basis of how good a wife they were. Shirley Eskapa comments that any woman who is 'promoted' to a wife believes that in some important way she is superior to her predecessor. It appears that one of these ways is as a wife. This stepmother comments that her partner was driven from his family by the insensitivity his first wife showed to his needs at the end of a tiring day at work:

'It wasn't a happy marriage. He'd come home from work and the kids would be screaming and the place would be a wreck. He said he couldn't stand it.'

This stepmother describes her predecessor quite simply as lazy:

'As far as I gather she's very much like she is now, lazy. She sat on her arse all day reading and only got up when John came in.'

It is interesting how women judge each other according to those traits we saw in Chapter Two were the basis of women's role in society – being a good wife and mother. This suggests that we cannot see women as people at all. They are just wives and mothers. Nothing more. If they are not good at that then they must be no good altogether.

This leaves me thinking how unfair this is. We don't judge the worth of a man on whether or not he's good at his paid work. My dustman is a very poor dustman. He drops litter all over my garden and leaves half of the rubbish in the bin. However, whilst I might think he's a pretty awful dustman this doesn't mean he must be a rather nasty person. Why, therefore, should we assume that because a woman is rather bad at mothering and wifehood (assuming that all the stories you have heard about her are true) she must be bad to the core? Isn't it a case of double standards, when women judge women with such harshness and cruelty?

However, we should not forget, as the title *Woman versus Woman* so aptly reminds us, that this is a competition. To win the competition one has to be superior to the other. So, of course, it is in the interests of one woman to see her most valued female skills of mothering and wifehood to be superior. What the second wife is saying, when she criticises her partner's ex, is that she is the better prize.

Nevertheless we also need to ask why women should be in competition with each other? My answer to that is because of the rationality of the competition. Most women work in low-paid jobs with few hopes of promotion. When children come along they give up work and find themselves extremely dependent, financially and emotionally, on their partner. It is their partner – a man – who gives them access to financial security and someone to share the trials of raising children. If they wish to return to work, to gain some financial independence, they rapidly find that the only work they can take has to fit in with children's needs and school hours. Their financial independence is partial at best. They still need a man to survive. So the prize is well worth having. He represents your financial future and your status. Have you ever considered your battle in this light or have you always thought it was at best a clash of personalities, at worst that your life had become entangled with a she-devil?

In addition, we must ask how we get to the position of seeing all these ex-wives as evil and nasty? Were they born that way or did it just happen?

HOW DOES THE EX GET TO BE SEEN AS WICKED IN THE FIRST PLACE?

This question requires us to have a rather dispassionate look at some of the processes of divorce and access visits which might lead us into thinking the worst of our enemies. These are:

● experiencing divorce;
● the post-divorce stage;

- remarriage or repartnering;
- children as go-betweens.

You may find that none of these stages is entirely separate in your own circumstances. For many, the stages and experiences of separation and divorce are far more interwoven. For our purposes here this does not matter. You will recognise your own experience as you read through.

Experiencing divorce

Divorce is set up as an adversarial process. This basically means that the previously married are pitched against each other as potential victor and vanquished. The spoils? The equity in the house, maintenance, any other goods and chattels, the children. The divorce process doesn't encourage you to be conciliatory. It is about ensuring you get your rights. These can obviously be diametrically opposed. So, whilst it is in the wife's interest to get as much maintenance as possible, it is in the husband's interests to pay the least. The battle begins and no holds are barred.

Your experiences of the 'other person' will be located in the reality of this adversarial process. This is how one stepmother described being on the receiving end of this:

'We received an affidavit from her [ex-wife] which was full of lies and filth. She accused my husband of some terrible things. He'd hit her. He'd accused her of being a prostitute. She raked up all this mud about some of their most private things.'

This is how one divorced man spoke of his experience:

'When we split up my wife screwed me for everything she could get. She works in a bank and had access on the computer to any of my accounts. I couldn't deposit money anywhere. She'd soon know about it and I'd get a solicitor's letter asking for her share. The final straw came when I had an accident in my car. It was written off and she even asked for half the insurance money saying it was half her car.'

Another divorced man I know described this situation:

'She [wife] turned round and threatened Wendy [his girlfriend]. She told her, "You've got no right to stay here and sign on the dole. That's illegal.' She was using it as a weapon.'

The result of these experiences leaves you angry and bitter. This can all too often spill over into any communication you have with your previous partner. It therefore becomes dangerous to extend contact for too long a period. It may also not be in your interests. If the 'other side' get to know too much about your current affairs, they might be able to use it against you!

These experiences also begin to seal some of the last vestiges of caring you may have had for your ex-partner. Your perception of them begins to change as you wonder what sort of person you really married. They are on their way to being 'wicked'.

The post-divorce stage

By this time you are, therefore, hardly speaking except when it is absolutely necessary. This is usually about the children, access visits and maintenance. Any vestiges of mutual respect have long since vanished. The need to stay in communication because of the children, however, is a problem. Talking directly to your ex risks arguments and scenes. You both carry too much bitterness about what has happened since the separation and it is unlikely you can speak to each other for long before an argument breaks out. Communication therefore becomes short and to the point as these post-divorce parents indicate:

'When we speak on the phone I keep to the bare details. Where and when I am going to see the children. Nothing more. I don't like talking to her so I keep it short.'

> 'When she brings the children for a visit I'm polite
> enough. But I don't encourage her in. We do the hand-
> over on the doorstep.'

> 'When he comes to pick up the children he stays in the
> car and I send them out. We don't speak at all.'

A new partner may also encourage a minimum of contact:

> 'I know John doesn't like me having anything to do
> with my first husband. He doesn't say anything but I
> know it makes him uncomfortable. I can't blame him. I
> don't want anything to do with him either.'

The lack of communication means that you do not have the
chance to build up any alternative image except the one that
your recent experiences have suggested are the correct ones.
The bad image of the malicious ex-wife.

Remarriage or repartnering

The arrival of a new partner is possibly the final nail in the
coffin as far as communication with an ex is concerned. For
one thing, your new partner is unlikely to want a close
association between you and your previous partner to
blossom. Rather, their inclination may be to keep it distant
and formal, even non-existent. It can be too threatening to
their sense of security for it to be otherwise. Your ex also
might be less than pleased that you have someone new in
your life. This is her replacement. There's no going back from
here. Besides, if it looks as if things are working out too well
for you there may even be twinges of jealousy and envy.

The stepmother's first-hand experience of the ex may also
confirm the stories she has heard from her partner or her own
other direct experiences of what an awful person the first
partner is:

> 'We got an affidavit from her on our wedding day.'

> 'We had a letter from her solicitor just before Christ-
> mas telling us that she was moving back into the house.
> We were living there with the children. She didn't

want the children though really. She wanted the house. She was using the children as a way of getting the house back. She walked out on them but soon realised where her bread was buttered.'

Current wives are not the only ones who have a few tales to tell about the ex-wife. Their husbands also join in the tirade about a previous spouse and the risks entailed in communication. Non-communication can be a way of protecting yourself from the risks of confrontation. As this father points out, it can also stop you being blamed for any mishap:

'Everybody when they first meet Jane [ex-wife] think she's really nice. Until they get to know her. Even when times were arranged to see the children and after numerous promises the event of her turning up was a rarity. I keep out of having anything to do with the arrangements because when she makes promises to the kids and breaks them they'll see it's her fault. Not mine. She's not a mother. She's an excuse.'

You are enmeshed, therefore, in a situation which tells you that the least contact the better for all concerned. But those children still need to be seen. You still need to know how they are getting on at school or whether they are going on holiday this summer with their mother or not. You still, therefore, need to talk.

The go-between stepchildren

All books on the stepfamily tell you not to use children as go-betweens. In particular, it is unfair on the children as you are exposing them to concerns about where their loyalty lies. Whilst you ask them to take messages about dates and times of visits, you also question them about what is going on in the 'other' house they visit. 'Is that man living with her?' 'Has she got a new job that pays more money?' This can make your children feel disloyal. It can make them feel they are 'telling tales'. They are stuck in the middle, just like the unfortunate men we considered in Chapter Three.

Nevertheless, there is no doubt that children are extremely useful as go-betweens. In particular, they allow you to continue the necessary communication with their other parent without risking the consequences. You do not risk a row, an argument, a scene. In my own research, children were frequently used as go-betweens for this reason. Communication, if it had not totally broken down between their parents, was incredibly risky. So children carried messages about pocket money, dates and times of access visits and what that parent was currently up to. Whilst I wholeheartedly agree with the moral argument that children should not be in the position of go-between, given their value it is unlikely that stepparents will cease using them in this way.

However, whilst children are no doubt useful in this role, the problem with this form of communication is that it does not always give you accurate information. Mostly, the information you receive is partial at best, wrong at worst. If the moral argument doesn't convince you, perhaps this one will. Children are the intermediary and the danger with all intermediaries is that some important piece of information will be lost, or indeed never heard in the first place, or be reported as quite different to the reality of what took place.

This can mean that the views you have already formed since divorce or remarriage never really have to be challenged. These are the confirming tales that some children have told their parent and stepparent. You will see how they confirm the bad image of their mother, however inadvertently this might be on the part of the child:

'Whenever they stop with her, and in ten years they've never stopped longer than two days, every night's a take-away. She never cooks for them. You'd think she'd get the culinary skills out when they go and stay.'

'I think the worst was on the night of his [stepson's] birthday. She went to a pop concert without telling him and left him there alone.'

'They tell me she's promised them a present and then she tells them she left it on the bus. I know she's lying. She's not honest with them at all.'

'We know, from what they say, that she's been talking about the past with them but she makes it untrue. They think she's just talking about the past but she's putting it from her point of view.'

'Lots of little stories have come back and we think "*that's* a way to behave!" She'll give them joss sticks, and she's got kids' rainbow covers on her bed.'

We can see how each of these comments says something very negative about the ex-wife as a mother to her children. They confirm everything that has been learnt about her in the preceding months and years. In just the same way that we considered in Chapter Five that we build confirming pictures of our stepchildren as wicked, so the same process will confirm that an ex-wife is wicked. Through being combatants in a divorce, you have become enmeshed in a process that creates its own logical outcomes.

As adversaries you have to act to protect your self-interest. This means that you will act in ways that may be less than nice and less than moral. You will have to hand many stories that confirm that your previous partner is a rather nasty piece of work. Turning the previously married into combatants also leads to wrath and anger. The logic of dealing with this is avoidance. Using children as go-betweens is the rational answer to avoiding conflict, yet using them can reinforce the attitudes that have been created by divorce.

Where does this leave us? Is the ex truly wicked or is it force of circumstances? Well, none of this is to say that the ex is not all the things you think she is. She may well be. No one is truly forced into acting in abominable ways and we should never forget there is always the element of choice. Possibly, however, it just seemed appropriate to her at the time.

What I have introduced here for you is the element of doubt. I return to my previous statements about this kind of issue. Can all ex-partners be evil, all stepchildren nasty, all stepmothers wicked? It is just not rational. Therefore, is there something in the way we interact with each other which leads us to think these things?

If you have trouble with an ex, it won't help you much to be told that you might have got it wrong. It's not something I would want to hear. However, if having trouble with an ex is destroying your life in some way, the following activity will help you break out of the cycle. The activity is designed to help you identify some of the reasons for your concerns:

ACTIVITY

DEALING WITH THE WICKED EX

Think through the following questions:

- Did you recognise any of your own experiences in the description of the stages from divorce to using children as go-betweens? Think through your own situation. What stories have you got to tell? How do they confirm that your view of the ex is correct? Is there any doubt?

- Ask yourself why dealing with your ex is so difficult. Do they seem to have some control over your life, such as the timing of access visits? Do they just make you angry at the sight of them?

This is an important activity. It will help you identify some of the causes for your feelings about an ex.

Depending on the outcome of your answers here, you might like to consider the following courses of action:

- **Talk directly to the ex.** This will be the hardest thing in the world but, as you will have seen, many of your ideas about them will have been the result of not communicating. Keep it short and to the point. Start with something very uncontroversial. Even a simple comment about the weather may break the ice and can be something you can work on over the coming months. My partner's divorce went on for some years as the solicitors' letters were tossed back and forth. It was not until he and his first wife actually talked to each other directly about the settlement that anything got sorted out. It was an expensive lesson to learn.

- **Get some control in your life.** Don't always feel at the mercy of others. If some of your problems result from a feeling that the ex is in control of your life, now is the time to take some positive action. Talking is one! Be more assertive, for example, about the dates and times of access visits. Don't let them always be in the driving seat whilst you find your whole life geared around the ex's demands. It doesn't do your self-esteem any good. One couple I know feel they have taken some control in their lives through not allowing an ex-partner access to their new home. They want to keep her out of their lives as much as possible and keeping her out of the house is a symbolic way of achieving this.
- **Minimise entanglement.** The idea of a clean break is an excellent one to give couples a fresh start. Where there are children this is much more difficult to achieve. However, you might like to use the idea of a clean break to look at the various ways your life is still intertwined with the past. Are there any steps you can take here to reduce this without your stepchildren suffering?

Remember: Ex-partners are like stepchildren. As they get older they become less of an interference in your life.

Dealing with a partner's ex can often be more difficult than dealing with stepchildren. It becomes another area of your life which is fraught with problems. But if those who are alive and well are a problem, what about those who have left this earth?

DEALING WITH THE GHOST OF THE DEAR DEPARTED

One of the stepfathers in my own research would give me many instances of the times his wife, now deceased, intervened in his and his partner's parenting of his children. He would find that things had mysteriously disappeared, only to reappear the next day. Items would move. This, he was convinced, was when his departed spouse was disturbed at some decision they had made about the children. It was not until they changed that decision that they thought the ghost would leave them alone. This story is really one about living with the ghost. They all felt that the ghost of the first wife continued to control their lives in very real ways and decisions were often made according to this.

How, therefore, do you live with a ghost? As we discussed in Chapter One, ghosts acquire saint-like qualities that can never be tested. It is an image that is very difficult to live up to and very irksome to think we may be compared with someone we probably did not know and certainly cannot see. Glynnis Walker, in her book *Second Wife, Second Best*, describes this as a no-win situation because if you say anything about it, it may be held against you. To criticise the dead is not allowed; even to criticise them obliquely is taking risks. So most women keep quiet, and smoulder silently inside.

Stepmothers in this situation may look for signs that the departed mother was not so brilliant as all would say. They may try to outdo her. One stepmother in my own study organised a wedding for her stepdaughter who had become pregnant. She went to great lengths to make it an occasion to remember. A relative who attended told her that her stepdaughter's mother would not have done so much for her. Rather, she would have taken a very dim view of the fact that her daughter had become pregnant before marriage and any celebration would have been a very quiet affair indeed. The superstepmom, however, has to prove her worthiness to the world whether the mother is alive or dead.

If you find living with a ghost is making life hard to bear, you might find some of the following tips helpful. We cannot challenge a ghost, but we can start by reaffirming our own worth.

TIPS FOR BEATING THE GHOSTLY BLUES

- **Start by remembering that no one's perfect**. Trite but true. It may help you to think about the negative stories you have heard as a way of helping you to come to terms with this fact. Although no one speaks ill of the dead, some snippets will come to you which will suggest that the deceased person was not all that everyone would have you believe.
- **Let off steam**. Have a good old moan with someone who is not a member of your or their family! Let off steam once in a while in a safe place. It'll do you good.
- **Try to be yourself.** I know this is a difficult thing to do but don't try to live up to a ghost. It's impossible. You are you and worthy in your own right. Don't pressurise yourself into having to think you have to be perfect. It is a total waste of your energy.
- **Don't allow your decisions to be influenced** by what 'they would have done if they'd still been here' or 'would have wanted'. Whilst of course you need to be sensitive, no one knows what they would have done in particular circumstances and when dealing with certain problems. You have to act on your own responsibility not through a ghost.

Remember: You're here. They're gone. Respect their memory but live your own life.

REVIEW

The key messages of this chapter are:

- moving into 'their' house needs tact and diplomacy;
- an 'our' child is a major decision that should not be taken lightly;
- the wicked ex-wife may not be so wicked;
- dealing with an ex, whether alive or deceased, can be as hard as parenting their children.

Remember: A second marriage might be distinctive. It can also be the best.

6

DID YOU KNOW...?

Do you know ... how the law regards stepparents?
Do you know ... how the law might regulate child maintenance payments?
Do you know ... the tax rules with regard to maintenance payments?
Do you know ... if you are entitled to state benefits?

Well ... did you?

This chapter is about enabling you to say, 'Yes, I did know.' Too often we neglect legal and financial issues in our lives. Only when the situation is pressing do we feel the need to find out. Often, by that time, it is too late to do much about it. 'If only I'd known,' you cry. I know. I have said the same!

This chapter is not a guide to legal and financial issues although certainly some of the information contained in this chapter will be useful at a factual level. I am not a legal nor a financial expert as many of my friends will testify. My advice would always be to check out your own personal situation with the appropriate professionals. Situations vary so much and so does the right solution.

This chapter is really a consciousness-raising exercise! It suggests that there are legal and financial implications for the stepfamily that you should be aware of. You should read the chapter in this spirit therefore. It may tell you things you did not know. It will also lead you to think that if you didn't know this, how much more is there that you don't know and may need to?

The details of the chapter focus on the British system. I hope, nevertheless, that readers in other countries will find the checklists just as useful. They will prompt you to think how the law, taxation and social security systems of your country deal with similar issues. My message is – find out!

There are two principles we need to understand when looking at the legal and financial areas of stepparenting:

- an understanding that whilst we view our stepfamily relationships as private issues, there is a public side to this. This public side is the way that legislation and public policy affect stepfamilies, stepparents and stepchildren;
- an understanding that our rights as parents and stepparents have to be balanced with the rights and needs of our children and stepchildren.

STEPFAMILIES AND THE LAW

For many stepfamilies, their experience of legal matters arises from their contact with a solicitor and courts during their divorce. For many, this experience was less than happy and less than satisfactory. One stepmother in my own research study considered that her husband was able to obtain better legal advice than she was as he had more money to spend on this. This left her with an ongoing sense that she had been cheated in the divorce settlement.

What appears to happen to most of us is that we do not think of the legal implications of any of our acts. This stepmother, in my view, was not only 'cheated' by her husband's ability to employ expensive counsel, but she was also probably 'cheated' by her own actions. Before the divorce came to court she had met her future husband. In the court's view, therefore, there was always the possibility that her maintenance and future financial needs would be met by the new man in her life. The court may, therefore, have taken this into account in the decisions on the divorce settlement. Had she known this before the divorce went to court, perhaps she would have been more cautious about how much of her new life she opened up to her ex-husband. She may well have kept her partner-to-be out of the picture until the legal process had been completed. As the police apparently say when you are arrested, 'Anything you say will be written down and used against you.' The fact that this stepmother was settled with another man could certainly have gone against her.

Stepmothers are not, of course, the only ones who feel that they have come out of a divorce financially worse off. Many men consider this is their experience as well. The son of a neighbour of ours married a few years ago. To mark the marriage, the father gave his son an equal partnership in his farm. Recently the couple separated and are going through a divorce. The wife, or daughter-in-law in this case, has asked for her share of the farm as part of the divorce settlement, as it forms part of her joint assets with her husband. Our neighbour now bitterly regrets giving his son half his farm as he now thinks he faces losing it from the family altogether.

These tales suggest that we need to know quite clearly the legal implications of our actions. Hopefully, your own legal needs have now ended, except perhaps to engage a solicitor to do your house conveyancing or to write your will. However, as we never know what awaits us, you might like to update yourself on some of the current legal issues facing stepfamilies today. In this section we shall look at:

- legislation concerning parents' responsibilities towards children;
- adoption and name change;
- wills;
- how the law protects children.

DO YOU KNOW WHAT YOUR LEGAL POSITION AS A STEPPARENT IS?

We have, throughout much of this book, talked about the ambiguous role of the stepparent. Nowhere can we see that more clearly than in relation to the legal position of the stepparent. As Elizabeth Hodder said in her book *The Stepparents' Handbook*, 'a stepfamily acquires a large number of duties, responsibilities and obligations (property, children, money) but has very few "rights".' This discrepancy between duties and rights has caused much concern among stepfamily members.

For example, in Britain, a stepfather, on divorce from a second marriage, can be held to be responsible for the financial maintenance of the stepchildren he acquired during that marriage. This can particularly be the case when such a child has been seen to be a 'child of the family' in legal terms. This is where both partners of a marriage have treated a child in this way. Yet, a stepparent does not have a 'right' in law to maintain contact with or continue to live with a child in the event of divorce or death of a spouse.

For many this is seen to be unfair. Also, it can jeopardise commitment amongst family members. How many stepfathers, for example, may be put off from offering financial support if they thought of this in terms of likely penalties.

THE 1989 CHILDREN ACT

There was hope that new legislation, in the form of the 1989 Children Act, might solve some of these anomalies. Is this the case? How are stepparents affected by the Children Act? We shall review the Children Act by looking at the idea of parental responsibility and the options for stepparents.

Whilst it is still early days yet for the Act to be working and setting legal precedents, as Judith Masson points out in an article entitled 'Stepping into the Nineties: a summary of the legal implications of the Children Act 1989 for stepfamilies' (printed in *A Step in Both Directions? The Impact of the Children Act 1989 on Stepfamilies*, edited by Brian Dimmock), the term stepparent is not used in the 1989 Act. Accordingly, as Judith Masson says, 'The Act gives stepparents no special rights and imposes no new responsibilities on them automatically . . . it imposes no financial obligations on stepparents but they remain liable to support their stepchildren following marriage breakdown.' The concern that the ambiguity of the stepparent's position remains is echoed by Donna Smith when she comments in the foreword to Dimmock's book 'there is still no approved institutionalised role for stepparents'.

Parental responsibility

The 1989 Children Act is by far the most important piece of recent legislation in relation to children in Britain. It focuses on the rights of children and the family of first marriage. The concept underpinning the Act is that of parental responsibility. This is defined by Section 3 of the Act as:

all the rights, duties, powers, responsibilities and authority which by law a parent of a child has in relation to the child and his property.

What is the parent responsible for? This definition of responsibility is obviously very general. Family life is too complicated for an Act of Parliament to set out everything that parents can or should do in every situation. However, the responsibilities are generally taken to include financial, educational and medical responsibilities, to protect a child from physical and moral harm and to maintain contact with the child.

In addition to what a parent's responsibilities are, the question for stepfamilies is, which parent is responsible? The Act predominantly focuses on the responsibility of the child's natural parents:

- for a child born to married parents the responsibility belongs to both parents;
- for a child born to unmarried parents, the responsibility belongs exclusively to the mother.

Unmarried fathers can acquire parental responsibility in two ways. Firstly, when the natural parents agree, they put this agreement in writing in a prescribed form called a 'parental responsibility agreement'. This is recorded in the Principle Registry of the Family Division. Secondly, the father can apply to court. The court can order that responsibility be shared by mother and father.

The options for stepparents

Where does all this leave stepparents? For example, one of the issues that concern stepparents is what happens to their relationship with the stepchildren in the event of their spouse's death:

- How can they make their position with regard to their stepchildren more certain?
- Can stepparents acquire parental responsibility?
- Will this solve these kinds of problems?

Stepparents can indeed acquire parental responsibility in several ways. Nevertheless, each of these pathways has a different status and should not be regarded as automatically solving any likely future stepparental concerns. The ways that a stepparent can apply for parental responsibility are:

- by being appointed a guardian of the child;
- through a residence order;
- through a care order;
- by adopting a child.

Each of these steps clearly has complex and varied legal implications attached to them. Take legal advice therefore if you think that you wish to pursue any of these options. However, before doing so you may want to think through some of the consequences of any action you take or do not take. The following questions will help you to think about this in relation to acquiring parental responsibility:

CHECKLIST

WILL ACQUIRING PARENTAL AUTHORITY
BENEFIT OUR SITUATION?

Ask yourself the following questions:

- Why do I want to acquire parental responsibility? Are the reasons connected to confirming a 'psychological bonding' with a stepchild or stepchildren or to secure 'rights' over a child or children?
- Are my concerns equal for all of my stepchildren?
- When? The stage you are at in your relationship with your stepfamily is a matter to be thought through very carefully. The early stages are particularly marked by that 'honeymoon' feeling. How well established are you in your relationship with your stepchildren?
- How? Which are the most appropriate steps to take to meet these needs?
- What rights do I acquire by following this course of action?
- What expectations are placed upon me?
- How does this affect my own situation?
- How does this affect my stepchildren's situation?
- How does this affect my spouse's position?
- How does this affect the non-resident parent's position?

Remember: Parental responsibility cannot be relinquished by a natural parent. It can be shared though.

DO YOU WANT TO CHANGE YOUR STEPCHILDREN'S NAMES?

We have discussed how important names can be in step-families. They can be a sign of commitment. They can be a way of uniting the family. They can enable the stepfamily to appear to the outside world as one. Stepfathers may very strongly want their stepchildren to carry their name. Step-children may wish to take a stepfather's name as a sign of their love for him. Stepmothers may want their stepchildren and their children to share the same name. When a child's mother marries and takes her new husband's name the child may feel excluded if her or his name is different. At an informal level, the change of children's surnames happens every day. Mothers simply register their child at a new school with their new married name.

However, many families want to formalise the name change. Indeed, they may be required to do so for a myriad of official reasons such as the issue of passports and opening building society accounts. There are various ways this can be achieved; a statutory declaration, which requires a solicitor or JP to witness your statement, or by deed poll.

In these cases you will require the natural father's consent. What happens if he objects? In the case of dispute, you can of course take the matter to court, who can make a decision in favour of either party. The decision you have to make is whether it is worth it.

The following questions might help you to think through some of the issues about name change – unofficial or official:

CHECKLIST

CHANGING STEPCHILDREN'S NAMES

Ask yourself the following questions:

- Is everyone, including the children, absolutely agreed that the change of name is for the benefit of all?
- Is anyone unhappy or objecting to the change – for example, grandparents, aunts and uncles?
- What do you see that a change of name will achieve – less embarrassment, a sense of unity, a sign of caring, etc.?
- Will changing a child's surname realistically achieve any or all of these?
- What are the psychological implications of changing a name? When I separated from my first husband, I reverted by statutory declaration to my maiden name. I felt very strongly I had regained myself. On my second marriage, I retained my maiden name for work, as I never wanted to lose my identity so much again, but took my husband's name out of love for him and my stepchildren. I wanted all of us, including our 'our' child, to have the same surname. It was a way of bonding all of us separate individuals, with our different histories, together as a family. Many step-children change their surname back to that of their biological father as a way of retrieving their psychological identity, their roots. Is this likely to be the case in your stepfamily?
- Is there any chance that the change of name is a cosmetic attempt to solve deeper problems? If so, it won't work.
- When should you take such a step? If you wait a long time it may seem pointless as you've managed for so long. If you do not wait, how sure can you be that the stepfather and stepchildren will get on?
- What happens if this marriage or relationship ends? How many changes of surname can your children have? Think of their school certificates or records of achievement. Is there any chance these will be in different names?

DO YOU WANT TO ADOPT YOUR STEPCHILDREN?

Adoption is often something considered by stepfamilies as a way of ensuring that a stepchild has the same legal rights as a natural child of the stepparent. Where there is an 'our' child, for example, the parent may feel that the stepchild is at a disadvantage. The stepchild will not automatically have the same inheritance rights as the 'our' child. The stepchild may feel in some way different or not as wanted. Adopting a child is certainly attractive as a way of sealing a relationship.

Adoption is a serious issue and should not be undertaken lightly. It should be seen as a permanent, life-long, commitment. As with the case of name changes, you need to question your motives very closely:

CHECKLIST

ADOPTION

Ask yourself the following questions:

- Why is adoption a good idea?
- Why do you think the child's other parent should give up their rights and responsibilities to their child or children?
- Search your heart. Are any of your motives to do with revenge, by seeking to obliterate the other parent from your lives?
- Ensure no coercion has occurred. Children can be very perceptive and may want to please you rather than thinking it's a good idea in itself.

There are, of course, advantages and disadvantages to adoption which Elizabeth Hodder, in *The Stepparent Handbook*, sets out so admirably. These include:

- **Advantages:** the ending of problems associated with loyalty, the grass can no longer be greener because it is no longer an option; if the marriage breaks down, the stepparent has more rights in relation to the child than she or he would have done without adoption; children can feel more secure.

- **Disadvantages:** it destroys the ties the child has with a natural parent; an adopted child loses the rights to maintenance payments from the natural parent which can cause financial problems in the stepfamily; the child may feel they have 'lost' their other natural parent in quite a final way.

When thinking through the matter of adoption, you should bear the following points in mind:

- The court will be concerned about the welfare of the child – nobody else. This is paramount.
- The court will take into account the wishes of the child so far as this is possible in terms of the child's age and level of understanding.
- The child must live with the applicants before an application is made.
- The parents or guardian of the child must consent with full understanding and unconditionally to the adoption.
- Adoption completely severs the legal links a child has to their family of origin. This not only means the father or mother, but also the grandparents, aunts and uncles, etc. This is important to note with regard to inheritance, let alone the social and emotional matters.
- Adoption gives the stepparent the same rights, responsibilities and duties as a natural parent.

HAVE YOU MADE YOUR WILL?

Make a will. Sound advice but how many people do? Have you thought where your money and most precious belongings could end up if you die intestate, that is without having made a will? I have. My fear is that I will die and my husband will inherit. He will die and my stepchildren will inherit.

They will die and their mother will inherit. I'm afraid I wouldn't like that. At all!

Making a will is more than about ensuring that your money will not end up with the person you would least like it to. It also saves an awful lot of aggravation for your family after you've gone. At the very minimum, they will know what you would have wanted without having to second-guess or squabble. Here are some points to consider:

- as long as you are of 'sound mind' and, in the UK, have complied with the Wills Act 1837, you can dispose of your money as you see fit;
- remarriage revokes any will that has been previously made;
- in the case of intestacy, the surviving spouse is entitled to the estate to a set amount and the remainder is shared among the children of the deceased;
- couples who are not married have no right of inheritance from each other.

Note however that wills can sometimes be contested, though there may be strict time limits and restrictions on who can contest a will. If you are in any doubt, consult a lawyer.

Remember: Your inheritance really could end up where you would least like it to. Make that will!

STEPFAMILY FINANCE

Have you got money worries? Stepfamilies often do. The devastating effect that divorce can have on your financial situation can take some getting over. Divorce plunges many women and their children into the social security system where they remain for many years. As Jackie Burgoyne and David Clarke's study, *Making a Go of It*, indicates, many couples also literally inherit debts from an ex-partner. Many women indicate that they do not receive the maintenance they have been awarded and budgets are often extremely tight.

In addition to the financial complications of stepfamily life and the fact that there never seems to be enough to go round, as all commentators on the stepfamily note, money is used as a way of manipulating relationships. Fathers, for example, may see the payment of maintenance as a way of ensuring that they have the right to see their children. Mothers may be fearful that if they upset their ex-partner, he will refuse to pay vital maintenance. As we discussed in Chapter Three, the existence of a financial tie with a previous partner can hinder the establishment of new relationships within the stepfamily.

In looking at stepfamily finances, our objectives are:

- to consider how new legislation in Britain will affect maintenance and the stepfamily;
- to encourage you to take a second look at your tax and social security situation.

Take a cool, hard look at your financial situation by reading on.

WHAT STEPPARENTS NEED TO KNOW ABOUT CHILD MAINTENANCE AND THE NEW CHILD SUPPORT ACT 1991

Whilst the Children Act is the most important legislation affecting children and parents, the Child Support Act is the most important legislation affecting child maintenance. It is a radical step aimed at reducing the extent to which the state supports lone parent and post-separation and divorce families. Fathers will now be vigorously pursued to ensure that non-custodial fathers pay towards the upkeep of their child. The Child Support Act puts into practice one aspect of parental responsibility: that of financial support. The Act set up the Child Support Agency which commenced work in April 1993.

The Child Support Agency

This is an administrative body, not a legal one. Its role will be to assess and administer the father's liability to child maintenance support. Therefore,

- child maintenance will be dealt with by the Child Support Agency, not the courts, except in very limited circumstances;

- the courts will still deal with the other financial details of divorce such as settlements over houses and maintenance for a wife.

How does The Child Support Act affect the stepfamily?

For those in the stepfamily, there is much concern that this Act will have some dire financial consequences. Brian Dimmock, in his chapter 'Left Hand, Right Hand, Cock-up or Conspiracy? Some reflections on stepfamilies and legislation' in his book, *A Step in Both Directions?*, comments that the danger to the stepfamily is that the Child Support Act gives precedence to the first family. This, he notes, is a change from previous views that a man's first duty was to look after the children he is currently living with.

Previous views have enabled individuals to break free of some of the ties of the past and have a chance to start again. It was thought that the man's resources should be used to support that family and if, consequently, he does not have sufficient to maintain his first family then this would be an appropriate role for the state.

However the Act appears to be reversing this through the application of a formula which includes an allowance for any subsequent biological or adopted children that a man may have, but does not include an allowance for any stepchildren that he might also be maintaining. Indeed, stepchildren will reduce the amount of housing costs the stepfather can claim and so they represent a double liability.

This may be bad news for stepfamilies who struggle enough financially. It is also certainly bad news for fathers whose ability to meet their obligations to their stepfamilies will be reduced.

SEPARATION, DIVORCE AND MAINTENANCE: SOME TAX ISSUES

Have you ever considered the question of how your tax position might be affected by separation and divorce? Do you know the situation with regard to maintenance payments? As with legal matters, you should always take advice from a professional if you are in any doubt about your personal situation. Some points you should consider:

- What is my tax position as a partner in a marriage?
- What is my tax position as a separated person?
- What is my tax position if I am living with my partner but am not married?
- What tax allowances can I claim for my children?
- If I am making maintenance payments to my ex-partner, can I get tax relief?
- If my ex-partner is paying me maintenance, do I have to pay tax on those payments?

In Britain, changes were made in the 1988 Budget which means that there are, in effect, two systems in operation, one which applies to orders made before the 1988 Budget and one which relates to orders made after the 1988 Budget. If your personal situation comes under the pre-1988 system and you think it is to your advantage to change to the current one, this is allowable under Section 39 of the 1988 Finance Act. However, what is advantageous to one party may not be advantageous to the other.

Remember: Check your tax position is working in your interests.

HAVE YOU CLAIMED ALL YOUR STATE BENEFITS?

Every year we hear two things. Firstly, that the cost of making welfare payments is prohibitive. As a country we cannot afford them and recent legislation has sought to make fewer and fewer people eligible. Women are by far the largest recipients of welfare payments; a key reason for this is their position of looking after children as a lone parent. In the UK, for about 67% of lone-parent families, the main source of income is welfare payments. Living on welfare means poverty. It especially means poverty for our children. A book entitled *Poverty, The Facts* by Carey Oppenheim, published by

The Child Poverty Action Group, estimates that there are around three million children in the UK living in poverty – that is, going without the things that most of us would regard as a necessity.

The second thing we hear about every year is that there are large amounts of welfare benefits which go unclaimed. Indeed, every so often the government will launch a mini campaign to encourage people to claim all that they can. The complexity of the welfare system is certainly something that is set against the success of this. Moreover, we know that no one will ever be well off on benefit. The system is designed to act as a safety net but to discourage rather than encourage.

Nevertheless, it may be in your interests to get to know the welfare system a little better. It may certainly be in your children's interests. If you cannot do it for yourself because of the stigma involved, do it for them.

You may be able to claim benefit for your children, or because you are a lone parent or widow. You may be able to get extra money because you have low earnings or are unemployed. There may be grants or loans available, or other benefits such as free prescriptions.

STATE BENEFITS: ACTION LIST

To help you get to know the benefits system a little more thoroughly try:

- contacting your local Citizens' Advice Bureau who may be able to put you in touch with someone who can check your situation;
- visiting your local library or picking up government leaflets at your post office or local social security office;
- obtaining booklets, pamphlets and guides to benefits and welfare rights published by voluntary organisations.

Remember: Knowing your rights to benefit may improve your stepfamily's financial situation.

REVIEW

The key messages of this chapter are:

- stepparents have few 'rights' in relation to their stepchildren;
- radical changes have been made to the child maintenance system in Britain. This has serious implications for the stepfamily's financial situation. Keep up to date with changing legislation;
- you must know your tax and legal situation. It matters;
- have you claimed all the benefits to which you are entitled?

Remember: Protect your stepfamily's interests. Raise your consciousness about the law and finance. Use the organisations and books in Chapter Seven. Get professional help if you think you need it.

7

WHERE TO GO FROM HERE

I've read this book, you say. Now where do I go from here?
The answer is simple. You continue the process of tackling
the problems you face. You do this by continuing the process
of your own self-development that I hope this book has
contributed to.

Our broad self-development is so important I cannot stress
it enough. We can focus too much on our stepfamily problems
as if they were unique to the stepfamily or the only ones we
have to confront. Throughout this book I have encouraged you
to think of your problems in a wider context. Of course there
are special problems to stepfamilies. However, the problems
we have with stepchildren can be just the same as we have
with our natural children. The problems your stepchildren
experience with you can be just the same as the problems they
would experience with their natural parent. There is a danger
that living in a stepfamily becomes an excuse, a scapegoat in
itself, for all your problems.

This final chapter takes this message one stage further. It
suggests that some of your problems could be solved by
extending your horizons, by looking beyond the stepfamily
and unlocking your potential more fully. We limit ourselves
every day by letting our problems get the better of us and by
thinking that we do not have the capabilities to change. You
do have that capability if only you will believe in yourself. So
be ambitious. Try some of the approaches to self-development I have included in this chapter, and some of those listed

in the organisations and books pages (pages 213–26). They will help you reach your potential, both as a stepparent and as a human being.

This chapter is designed to help you think about how you could start this wider self-development process. It does this by:

- discussing some alternative approaches to self-development;
- giving you the addresses of organisations and a book list which will help you follow up all of the issues raised in this book.

Let's take our final steps to successful stepparenting, and a successful life.

COUNSELLING AND THERAPY

Is your idea of therapy sitting on the psychiatrist's couch exploring your neuroses? Is it wrapped up in ideas that only rich American superstars go 'into therapy', usually for years and seemingly with little pay-off? Do you see it as something that would be embarrassing to admit to because people would think you couldn't cope with your problems? These are all very understandable ideas. We often think of therapy as only necessary for those who have deep mental problems, rather than to help you to cope with the everyday crises of life. Moreover, as I pointed out in Chapter One, I am also sceptical of some of the theories that underpin therapy approaches. Nevertheless, the proof of the pudding, as they say, is in the eating and my experiences of psychotherapy in particular certainly tell me 'there's something in it'!

My own knowledge of therapy has been through some research I contributed to for the Department of Applied Social Studies at the University of Warwick. This entailed interviewing women who had been through psychotherapy at a Women's Therapy Centre, where the focus of the work is to look at the women's childhood and past life as a way of understanding their current problems. What struck me most when I met the women I interviewed was how alive and energetic they were. They seemed to buzz with life. They also had a confidence and peace within themselves that said 'I'm OK'. Of course they still had problems in life. Who doesn't? But they had an inner resilience which enabled them to believe that these problems could be overcome.

The explanation for all this energy is that these women have been freed, through psychotherapy, of the psychological burden of the bad or poor experiences they had had in the past. Literally, a weight had been lifted from their minds which released a buzzing life-force. These women attributed their ability to say to themselves 'I'm OK' and really believe it to the understanding that psychotherapy had helped them to achieve being able to recognise appropriate and inappropriate feelings.

Meeting these women definitely changed my thoughts about the value of therapy but it also taught me two important things:

- there are different types of therapy;
- choosing the right approach for you is vital.

There are many types of therapy: Gestalt, feminist, psychotherapy, counselling and so forth. These different types rest on different theories or approaches to the problems the client has. For example, feminist psychotherapy rests on the idea that to understand, and help, the psychological problems which women have, you need to build on how being a second-class citizen affects women's mental health. Luise Eichenbaum and Susie Orbach, in their book *Understanding Women*, set out how women's psychology results from their having to cope with the following rules in society:

- women defer to others, follow their lead and articulate their needs only in relation to others. As a result women believe they are not important in themselves for themselves;
- women must always be connected to others and shape their lives in accordance with a man's. Women, therefore, feel odd if they don't have a man. As we saw in Chapter Three,

we don't have a positive image in our society of single women and never believe they are single out of choice;

- having to be connected to someone else means that women learn to anticipate others' needs and fulfil them. This means not only that their own needs come second but that they become hidden. As Eichenbaum and Orbach comment, women carry deep feelings of neediness.

The process of feminist psychotherapy rests on these ideas and understanding the mother–daughter relationship. When you engage in feminist psychotherapy, a lot of time can be spent exploring your relationship with your mother in particular.

This can be compared with the work of marriage guidance counselling which takes a broader focus, matching its clientele which, of course, includes men as well as women. As we saw in Chapter One, the main idea is the same, to look at your past family relationships and see how they relate to your present situation. However, the difference between counselling and therapy is mainly that whilst therapy focuses on the past, counselling will deal with more current issues.

In addition, these different types of counselling and therapy techniques can be organised in different ways. These can be:

- one-to-one work;
- work as a couple;
- work with the whole family;
- group therapy with others whom you will not know initially.

The type you choose will depend on what you feel is most appropriate and the emphasis of the organisation. Marriage guidance counsellors, for example, will work with you alone or with you and your partner together. Women's therapy centres mainly focus on the individual or use group work.

Choosing the right approach for you is the most important factor for therapy or counselling to be most successful. We all seek different things from counselling or therapy. The key is to match up your needs with what is on offer. Here are some factors to think about when choosing:

COUNSELLING AND THERAPY CHECKLIST

- **What type of therapy is for you?** Speak to the different organisations offering therapy (see list on pages 213–19) and ask them what their main approaches are.
- **Speak to the organisation about the best approach to your problems.** Ask them whether one-to-one, as a couple, as a family or in a group will be the most beneficial for you.
- **Think this through for yourself also.** One-to-one will give you an opportunity to focus on your own needs but will not create the same insights in others around you. You may find they have some resistance to the 'new you' because they haven't been through a similar process. Work as a couple or as a family can help you all to sort out common problems and consider how you relate to each other. Group work enables you to share similar experiences and use the group as support in understanding and changing your situation.
- **Think of the relationship with the counsellor or therapist as a contract.** You should have mutual respect and both be giving something to the relationship for it to work.
- **Cost is also a factor.** Most therapy can only be obtained privately and so you need to think of how much you can afford. Whilst I wouldn't say buying therapy is the same as buying a pound of bacon and you should find the best price available, there is no harm in comparing costs and having some idea what you are going to get for your money!
- **Time.** It is not unusual for people who have counselling and therapy to find that the whole process can take between six months and a year. The therapist will not be able to tell you exactly how long you will need, as it depends so much on a host of other factors including how often you have a session. This can be weekly, fortnightly or monthly and may also vary depending on what 'stage' you are at. You may want to have some discussion, however, with your therapist at the outset about the time implications, particularly as this will also affect the total cost of the therapy.

Remember: Engaging in therapy is not just for the rich and famous or for those with severe mental health problems. It could help you understand yourself and your life better.

ASSERTIVENESS TRAINING

If you know that therapy is not for you, or even if you think it is, another approach to changing your life could be through assertiveness training. Assertiveness is often confused with aggressive behaviour but these are very distinct. Assertiveness is, as Gael Lindenfield says in *Assert Yourself*, a way of behaving which helps us to communicate clearly and confidently our needs, wants and feelings to other people without abusing in any way their human rights. It is an alternative to passive, aggressive and manipulative behaviour.

Assertiveness is seen to be an area where both women and men can gain some control over their lives. As this extract from Herbert Fensterheim and Jean Baer's book *Don't Say 'Yes' When You Want to say 'No'* illustrates, assertiveness can indeed change your life. Jean Baer tells of how, before her husband Herbert Fensterheim helped her with assertiveness, she was timid and fearful. She felt her friends were always making demands on her, her family was always picking on her, she was fearful of losing her job. This is one way assertiveness helped to change Jean's life:

> **Re friends and family, he [Herbert Fensterheim] had this to say. 'You're so caught up in this need for being liked that you sacrifice your own self-respect. You could at least learn to handle put-downs in a way that makes you respect yourself. Now when friends and family criticise you, you just feel hurt and keep quiet, which is silent acquiescence which makes you hate yourself. A simple statement like 'I don't like what you've said' will change the whole picture. And maybe, eventually, you'll learn to turn criticism back on them, and they'll stop doing it ...**
>
> **As a result of this advice in just two years: ...**

> **I have learned how to answer my so-called friends who put me down with such remarks as 'Anybody could write the books you write – you just sit down and do them, that's all.' I progress from 'How can you speak to me like that?' to an assertive 'Jealous?'**

I doubt that assertiveness is the total cure-all that the authors of this book would lead us to believe in their evident enthusiasm. However, it is recognised by many people, including large organisations who run training courses in assertiveness for staff, that some change to your response patterns can help you to enhance your self-respect, self-confidence and self-worth and increase your effectiveness in life.

Some of the aspects of our behaviour that assertiveness is seen to help us with are:

- dealing with criticism;
- learning how to say 'no';
- dealing with anger;
- setting goals for yourself;
- coping with put-downs.

To give you an idea of some of the ways that assertiveness works, here is an outline from Anne Dickinson's book *A Woman in Your Own Right*. This deals with how to say that hardest word in the world 'no'. Why is it the hardest word? Because saying 'no' is often seen to be hurtful and selfish or rude and aggressive. When we say 'no' we are frightened that we will upset and hurt the other person. They will feel rejected by our 'no' or be angry with us. So we say 'yes' instead and then spend a lot of energy and time either trying to extricate ourselves from the situation or going through with it with heavy regret. We are annoyed with ourselves for having said 'yes' when we really mean 'no'! These are some of the steps you can take to learn to say that 'no', according to Anne Dickinson:

CHECKLIST

SAYING 'NO' ASSERTIVELY

1 **Notice your immediate reaction.** If it is a definite 'yes' or 'no' then it's probably no problem. You will respond accordingly. However, if you feel at all unsure about the request at all, try saying 'I don't know. I need some more information.' Do not be pushed. This helps you in two ways. It gives you some time to think about it a little more. The extra information may help you to decide. If you are being asked to take your mother shopping, for example, you can ask where she wants to go and how long it will take. These factors may help you decide.

2 **Practice saying 'no' without excessive apology or excuses.** One of the problems we have when we say 'no' is that we want to let people down gently. It leads to us going into convoluted explanations and abject apologies which are often unconvincing. Anne Dickinson reminds us that when you say 'no', you are refusing the request, not rejecting the person. This is important to recognise, as we normally think that a 'no' will be seen as a rejection of the person. A simple, clear statement of why you cannot accept is sufficient.

3 **Treat the other person as your equal.** Do not say 'yes' out of pity. Allow the person to express how they feel when you do say 'no'.

4 **Don't hang around at the end of the conversation.** When we feel bad about something, we hover or stay rooted to the spot, prolonging the agony. Don't. Say what you have to say and cleanly end the conversation.

5 **Acknowledge your own feelings by knowing that the reasons for saying 'no' are important to you**, say, because you need time to yourself, or you hate shopping with your mother. Acknowledge the other person's feelings as well. Accept that they may feel angry or disappointed but don't go on a guilt trip. You can help to avoid this by the acceptance of your own needs.

This brief outline of one aspect of assertiveness training will give you some indication of how it can help you in your life. If you think it will, the book list and organisations listed at the end of this chapter will help to get you started.

Remember: You have needs too. Assertiveness can help you meet these needs.

STRESS MANAGEMENT

Don't they say that stress is the biggest killer of all? We certainly hear a lot about stress-related diseases such as heart troubles, ulcers or alopecia and we hear about stress-related symptoms such as alcoholism, depression and anxiety states, even suicide. Some stress, however, can be beneficial. It can get that adrenalin going which helps us pass exams or solve problems in our lives. Stress is a type of pressure that can affect us emotionally and mentally. What we need, psychologists tell us, is a balance. Too much stress can lead to being unable to cope with even the simplest things. Too little, and we become inert and inactive.

Are you stressed? Here is a checklist of the signs that could tell you that you are.

ARE YOU STRESSED?: A SHORT CHECKLIST

Do you spent a lot of your time:

- being tired or listless?
- being angry or short-tempered?
- feeling depressed?
- in tears or feeling tearful?
- finding it hard to sleep?
- finding your heart beating faster than usual?

If you answer yes to one or more of these symptoms and you are finding that this is making life difficult to cope with, take some steps now. Here are some suggestions:

- **Identify the cause of your stress.** There are many factors that can cause stress: money worries, unemployment or pressure of work, health problems, partners, stepchildren. If there is an identifiable cause, can you take some steps to solving the problem?
- **Seek help or support.** Do not be afraid to ask for help if you feel it will be of use. Emotional and practical support can be invaluable in taking some of the pressure off you. Some of the organisations listed in this chapter may be able to provide you with a starting place for finding that support.
- **Try relaxation techniques.** We meet stressful situations every day in our family lives: your stepchildren getting you down; your ex not sending the maintenance payment; sorting out children's arguments; the washing machine flooding your kitchen. Relaxation techniques can help you cope from day to day. Try this: lie on the floor. Close your eyes. Tense every muscle in your body. Now consciously relax each muscle individually, starting at your toes and working up through your whole body. Every muscle needs to be relaxed. Lie in this relaxed state for 3–5 minutes. Now stir yourself gently. Open your eyes. Sit up very slowly. Now you can stand.

Remember: Get your stress levels in balance!

THE POSITIVE YOU: THE NEW YOU

Many of us live our daily lives wishing we could be more successful, wealthier, happier. We think in phrases such as 'If I was successful then life would be...' or 'If I had a good relationship with my stepchildren then...' or 'I wish I was a good stepfather then...'. The problem with this way of thinking is that your outlook becomes self-limiting. By saying 'if' or 'I wish' you are telling yourself that your dreams and hopes are not really possible. This is because words like 'if' and 'I wish' are usually followed by 'but'. The phrases become 'If I had a good relationship with my stepchildren then life would be great but ...' or 'I wish I was a good stepfather but ...' Your thoughts following the 'but' tell you the reason why you cannot realise your hopes. You sigh and do nothing. Your life remains unchanged.

Have you ever thought that if you changed the way you think about your problems this might help you to realise your dreams? That if you turned the 'If I had ...' to 'I do have ...' and the 'I wish I was' to 'I am' then you would be in a better position to achieve your hopes and goals? Don't 'I do have a good relationship' and 'I am a good stepfather' sound much more positive and hopeful? Much less indecisive? You might be surprised how much your outlook changes by thinking in this way rather than in more negative phrases.

This final activity asks you to list some of the goals you would like to achieve and to link them to positive phrases such as 'I am' and 'I do have'. It takes you no further. You have started to achieve some of those goals by reading this book. The organisations and books listed in the following pages will help you take that further. The objective of this final exercise is to lift your spirits a little, to let you think 'I can do it' rather than 'I wish I could'.

ACTIVITY

CREATING A POSITIVE OUTLOOK

1 Make a list of all the goals you would like to achieve in the next twelve months. For example, a good relationship with your stepchildren, getting rid of that 'wickedness' complex, getting rid of the idea that the stepfamily is a problem family, being a good parent, and so forth.

2 Write a positive statement against each goal using the phrase 'I am ...' or 'I have ...', *not* 'I would like to be ...' or any other indecisive phrase.
For example:
   ● I am a good stepmother
   ● I am a good stepfather
   ● I have a good relationship with my stepchildren
   ● I have a successful stepfamily
   ● I am a success at stepfamily relationships

3 Say these phrases to yourself every day. Feel your self-esteem rise and your perceptions of your situation change in a more positive way. By saying 'I am a good stepmother/stepfather', or 'I am a success at stepfamily relationships', rather than 'I would like to be ...', your confidence will rise and you will begin to act in ways that suggest that you are.

This is an important activity. It will help you to:

● change your attitude to yourself;
● change your attitude to your situation;
● achieve your goals.

Remember: A positive outlook can create a sunnier world.

A FINAL WORD

Books always seem to have a final section called 'A Final Word', don't they? The last pearls of wisdom from the author. Well, this one is different. It is not a final word from me but from my stepdaughter. While writing this book I asked her if she had any advice she could give me – a risky thing to do at the best of times because I know how far I've fallen short in my own stepmothering of her. Nevertheless, I was pleased I took the risk because she treated me very kindly and did not retort 'You must be joking' or anything similar. She was constructive and helpful and spared my feelings a lot. For that she has my undying gratitude.

It seems to me appropriate to end with the voice of the stepchild. They are our future and our self-worth is often wrapped up in how well we get on with them. This is the advice of one stepchild, Siobhan Walker. I am sure you will find it useful.

FROM THE HORSE'S MOUTH: ADVICE FROM A STEPCHILD

---

1 Communication is the first and most important step. As the stepparent, you may have worries about whether the children of your partner will accept you and what responsibilities you would have as a consequence. There is no hard and fast rule. The natural parent may be alive or dead, but either way the stepchild will be grieving for the loss of the family unit and security and will be resentful of more change, personified by the introduction of the stepparent.

2 It is necessary to bear in mind that all the worries you may have will be intensified in the stepchild, purely because they are not yet an adult and their worries are tinged with a feeling of impotence plus, perhaps, the added issue of puberty and consequential emotional imbalance.

3 The stepchild has been bereft of a permanent authority figure. Explaining your role and the child's role will give them limits to work in. Often the stepparent will obtain a better relationship with the stepchild by asking to be their friend/authority figure rather than replacement parent/authority figure.

4 Preparation is also important. For this, interaction between the partner and the stepparent is essential as the partner will know the child better. To an extent, both partners will be working in the dark as the new family unit will be an entirely new experience for *all* concerned.

5 The child's parent should introduce the stepparent slowly to the children, in such a way that the children do not feel threatened, e.g. in a small group of the partner's mutual friends, so that the children can get to know the stepparent from a distance at first and that they can see how the stepparent will fit into their lives.

6 No matter how much the partners wish to be together – physically and emotionally – it is better to go slow. This is especially important in decisions about the future stepparent staying overnight.

7 The natural parent, after letting the children know that she or he is embarking on a new relationship, ought to have a discussion with the children to find out how they feel about this new situation and to reassure them that they will still be as much loved, no matter who the parent chooses as a future partner.

8 Many children fear they will no longer be an important part of their parent's life. In their minds, it is a matter of course that their natural parents will love each other and still have time for them but any love given to a stepparent could be, in the child's mind, to the detriment of the love their parent gives to them.

REVIEW

The key messages of this chapter are:

- the stepfamily is not a problem family but a family with problems;
- there are many different approaches to solving these problems, some of which are counselling and therapy, assertiveness training, stress management and positive thinking;
- self-development is an important way of tackling stepfamily problems which can also enhance many other facets of your life;
- communicate with your stepchildren.

Remember: The key to change is understanding. I hope this book has helped you both to understand and change your life. You can do both. I believe in you. Now believe in yourself.

ORGANISATIONS

UNITED KINGDOM

STEPFAMILY

The National Stepfamily Association
72 Willesden Lane
London NW6 7TA

Tel: 071 372 0844 (Enquiries and membership)
    071 372 0846 (Counselling)

Publishes newsletters, booklists and offers telephone counselling. Some members have set up local support groups. The only organisation in the UK devoted to stepfamily issues, the National Stepfamily Association, is a source of expert help, keeping up to date with the latest issues which are relevant to stepfamilies.

FAMILY THERAPY, COUNSELLING, CONCILIATION AND ADVICE

The British Association for Counselling
1 Regents Place
Rugby CV21 2PJ

Tel: 0788 578328

Send an A5 stamped addressed envelope for information on a number of services including a list of counselling organisations and therapists in your area, a counselling and psychotherapy resource directory for the whole of the UK and training requirements and opportunities

Cruse Bereavement Care
Cruse House
126 Sheen Road
Richmond
Surrey TW9 1UR

Tel: 081 940 4818

National organisation for the bereaved. Offers support and literature. Check your telephone directory for your local group.

Divorce Conciliation and Advisory Service
38 Ebury Street
London SW1W 0LU

Tel: 071 730 2422

Can offer help, conciliation and support for divorcing couples.

Families Need Fathers
134 Curtain Road
London

Tel: 071 613 5060

An organisation offering support and advice for fathers separated from their children after divorce.

Family Mediation Scotland
40 Shandwick Place
Edinburgh EH2 4RT

Tel: 031 220 1610

Conciliation service for divorcing couples.

Gingerbread
35 Wellington Street
London WC2E 7BN

Tel: 071 240 0953

Self-help group for single parents, organises social occasions and support. Offers advice and information to lone parents. Check your telephone directory for your local branch.

Parentline Network
44–46 Caversham Road
London NW5 2DS

Tel: 071 485 8535

Helps parents cope with everyday parenting problems.

Relate National Marriage Guidance
Herbert Gray College
Little Church Street
Rugby CV21 3AP

Tel: 0788 573241

Offers counselling for couples (whether married or not) and individuals. Can have long waiting lists and some contributory payment welcomed. Find your local branch in your telephone book.

Relate Marriage Guidance Northern Ireland
76 Dublin Road
Belfast BT2 7HP

Tel: 0232 323454

As above.

Women's Therapy Centre
6–9 Manor Gardens
London N7 6LA

Tel: 071 263 6200

Provides psychotherapy from a feminist perspective. Also has publications.

STEPFAMILY AND WORK

Combining family and paid work has never been easy. The following organisations may be of help to you if you experience difficulties here.

New Ways to Work
309 Upper Street
London N1 2TY

Tel: 071 226 4026

Advice about job share and flexible work patterns.

The Working Mothers Association
77 Holloway Road
London N7 8JZ

Tel: 071 700 5771

Provides information and support for working mothers (and stepmothers) and informal support through local groups.

HEALTH

As we commented in Chapter Two, living in a stepfamily can cause particular stresses. If you feel you need advice about your health, the following organisations may be able to help you.

Al-Anon Family Groups
61 Great Dover Street
London SE1 4YF

Tel: 071 403 0888

Support for family and friends who are concerned about a problem drinker.

Alcoholics Anonymous
PO Box 1
Stonebow House
Stonebow York YO1 2NJ

Tel: 0904 644026

Support for those who wish to stop drinking. Local groups and promise of anonymity.

British Acupuncture Association
22 Hockley Road
Rayleigh Essex SS6 8EB

Acupuncture can help with many health problems. Contact for information and advice.

National Association for Pre-menstrual Syndrome
PO Box 72
Sevenoaks Kent TN13 3PS

Support groups and help for those suffering from PMS. Send a stamped addressed envelope for details.

Women's Alcohol Centre
66 Drayton Park
London N5

Tel: 071 226 4581

For those who are concerned about the effect of alcohol in their lives. Offers local support groups.

LEGAL AND WELFARE ADVICE

British Agencies for Adoption and Fostering
11 Southwark Street
London SE1 1RQ

and

23 Castle Street
Edinburgh EH2 3DH

For those stepparents thinking of adoption, BAAF will be an invaluable resource.

Child Poverty Action Group
1–5 Bath Street
London EC1V 9PY

Publishes two excellent guides to the welfare benefits systems which are updated each April. These are *National Welfare Benefits Handbook* and *Rights Guide to Non-Means-Tested Benefits*.

Child Support Agency
PO Box 55
Brierley Hill
West Midlands DY5 1YL

Tel: 0345 133 133

Advice and information about how the Child Support Act may affect your child maintenance situation.

Citizens' Advice Bureaux

If you need legal advice about on-going post-separation and divorce problems or wish to make a will or are thinking about adoption but don't know where to start, you may find it worthwhile contacting your local Citizens' Advice Bureau. They keep lists of solicitors and are able to offer free information and advice on many issues. Your telephone directory will have the address and telephone number of your local office.

DSS Information Division (Leaflets Unit)
Block 4
Government Buildings
Honeypot Lane, Stanmore
Middlesex HA7 1AY

For leaflets and information about social security benefits.

DSS Helplines: For general advice on benefits

Tel: 0800 666 555 (England)
    0800 289 011 (Wales)
    0800 616 757 (Northern Ireland)

Solicitors' Family Law Association
PO Box 302
Keston, Kent

Tel: 06898 50227

Will be able to give you the names of local solicitors who are members of the Family Law Association, who take a non-adversarial approach to legal disputes concerning the family.

CANADA

Family Service Canada
55 Parkdale Avenue
Ottawa KIY 4GI

The Vanier Institute of the Family
120 Holland Avenue
Ottawa KIY 0X6

The United Church House
85 St Claire Avenue
Avenue East
Toronto 7 Ontario

AUSTRALIA

Anglican Marriage and Family Counselling Services
PO Box 1289
West Perth, Western Australia 6005

Australian Institute of Family Studies
300 Queen Street
Melbourne 3000
Victoria

Canberra Marriage Counselling Service Inc
PO Box 55
15 Hall Street
Lyneham ACT 2602

Marriage Reconciliation Separation and Family Counselling
262 Pitt Street
Sydney, New South Wales 2000

Useful books

This is not an exhaustive list of all the books available but they may help you get started in a wide range of areas. The asterisked books are those to which reference has been made in this book.

STEPFAMILY LIVING

*Jacqueline Burgoyne and David Clark (1984), *Making a Go of It, A Study of Stepfamilies in Sheffield*, London, Routledge and Kegan Paul.

The first British research study of the stepfamily and one which stands the test of time. Some thought-provoking quotes from the stepparents who took part in the study.

*Cherie Burns (1987), *Stepmotherhood*, London, Piatkus.

Very lively and straightforward. A good read and gets straight to the point.

Erica De'Ath (1988), *Step-parenting*, London, Family Doctors Publication.

Short booklet packed full of advice.

*Stephen Collins (1988), *Stepparents and their Children*, London, Souvenir Press.

Advice book containing 'Ten Principles of Stepparenting'.

*Brian Dimmock (ed.), *A Step in Both Directions? The Impact of the Children Act 1989 on Stepfamilies*, London, National Stepfamily Association.

A collection of chapters by different authors commenting on the effects of the 1989 Children Act for the stepfamily. Includes legal and welfare issues.

*Shirley Eskapa (1984), *Woman versus Woman*, London, Pan.

The battle between mistress and wife is exposed in this book and has parallels with second wife/first wife issues.

*Elsa Ferri (1984), *Stepchildren, A National Study*, London, NFER-Nelson.

Not one for the casual reader, this book contains a statistical analysis of data on stepchildren. Includes the effect on children of living in a stepfamily, in relation to education, behaviour and health.

*Deborah Fowler (1992), *Loving Other People's Children*, London, Vermilion.

An advice book with some interesting case histories. Thoughtful, with some excellent insight into the issues which really aggravate stepparents.

*Helen Franks (1988), *Remarriage, What Makes it, What Breaks it*, London, Bodley Head.

Charts from the end of the first marriage to considering the implications of the second. Again, some helpful advice.

*Elizabeth Hodder (1985), *The Stepparents' Handbook*, London, Sphere.

Elizabeth Hodder was the founder of the National Stepfamily Association and the person who gave me permission to use the *Stepfamily Newsletter* as a way of contacting stepparents for my own research study – for which I've always been eternally grateful! This is one of the first advice books for stepparents, written using Elizabeth's wealth of experience of stepfamily living. Still a good read.

Elizabeth Hodder (1989), *Stepfamilies Talking*, London, Optima.

This book gives the life histories of ten couples whom Elizabeth Hodder interviewed. Excellent for insight into other people's lives and knowing that you are not quite so alone with your own problems.

*Phillip Hodson (1984), *Men*, London, BBC.

Asks men to confront the issues raised by women's liberation, divorce and economic change. Asks men to establish a new male identity more relevant to modern times.

*Christina Hughes (1992), *Stepparents: Wicked or Wonderful*, Aldershot, Gower.

My own research on the stepfamily, based on studying five stepfamilies for a twelve-month period. Details their lives and the changes in them over this period. Forms the basis for many of the perspectives included in this book.

*Charlie Lewis (1986), *Becoming a Father*, Milton Keynes, Open University.

Discusses the role of men as fathers and how fatherhood affects men and family life.

*Brenda Maddox (1980), *Stepparenting: How to live with other people's children* (previously *The Half-Parent*, published 1975), London, Allen and Unwin.

This book has a special place in my heart as it was the first book I read about stepfamily life and I owe it a lot! It was wonderful to read about the experiences of other stepparents and to hear how similar they were to my own. Brilliant, readable and highly recommended.

*Donna Smith (1990), *Stepmothering*, London, Harvester Wheatsheaf.

Draws on the high expectations placed on stepmothers and the difficulties they face. Excellent for stepmothers in confirming how many of their difficulties are shared with others in the same situation.

*Glynnis Walker (1984), *Second Wife, Second Best? Managing your marriage as a second wife*, London, Sheldon Press.

As the title suggests, this book focuses on the particular difficulties that second wives face. Includes some stepfamily issues and a good resource for understanding your situation as a 'second'.

T Whelan and S Kelly (1986), *A Hard Act to Follow: Stepparenting in Australia Today*, Penguin.

An excellent title which sums up how many stepparents may feel, this book is based on interviews with stepparents and their children to get an inside view of the stepfamily.

DIVORCE AND CHILDREN

Edward Beal and Gloria Hochman (1993), *Adult Children of Divorce, How to achieve happier relationships*, London, Piatkus.

Written by an American psychiatrist and a professional writer, the book includes case histories and practical exercises. Examines what happens at the crucial points of marriage and parenthood for adults who experienced their parents' divorce.

*Ann Mitchell (1985), *Children in the Middle, Living through Divorce*, London, Tavistock.

A research study about children's experiences of divorce and separation. Not for holiday reading but excellent if you want to know how your children might really be feeling.

*Judith Wallerstein and Sandra Blakeslee (1990), *Second Chances*, London, Corgi.

An American study of children ten years after their parents divorced. Again, not light reading but was pathbreaking for being the first to research children in a long-term way.

Laurence Brown and Marc Brown (1986), *Dinosaurs Divorce, A Guide for Changing Families*, London, Collins.

Cartoon book for young children about divorce and visiting parents.

PARENTING

Don't forget stepparents face the same problems all parents experience. These books are not concerned with stepfamily life in particular but general parenting issues.

*Hilary Graham (1993), *Health and Hardship in Women's Lives*, Harvester Wheatsheaf.

Definitive text on women's lives.

A Katz (1992), *The Juggling Act, Working Mothers Share Their Experiences*, London, Bloomsbury.

If you are a working stepmother, this is for you.

S Kitzinger (1992), *Ourselves as Mothers*, London, Transworld Publishers.

Helps you understand the 'mother' part of your stepmother role.

*Penelope Leach (1979), *Baby and Child*, Harmondsworth, Penguin

Classic text on bringing up babies.

R Maxwell (1991), *Kids, Alcohol and Drugs*, Ballantine Books.

May be useful if this is a concern of yours.

J Melville and Dr F Subotsky (1992), *Does My Child Need Help? A guide for worried parents*, London, Optima.

For general concerns about parenting and identifying causes of problems.

FAMILY THERAPY AND PSYCHOTHERAPY

*Luise Eichenbaum and Susie Orbach (1983), *Understanding Women*, London, Penguin.

Widely quoted and easy to read. Based on feminist psychotherapy, this book helps you to understand some of the psychological problems you may face, including relationship problems, depression, phobia and eating disorders.

*Sarah Litvinoff (1993), *The Relate Guide to Starting Again: How to learn from the past to give you a better future*, London, Vermilion.

Advice book based on family therapy work. Includes activities and helps you understand and cope with the ending of relationships.

Robin Skynner and John Cleese (1983), *Families and How to Survive Them*, London, Mandarin.

A classic bestseller on family therapy. Question-and-answer style aims to help the reader understand the basis of their family problems.

Robin Skynner and John Cleese (1993), *Life and How to Survive It*, London, Methuen.

Sure to be another classic but a broader focus than their original work.

Joan Woodward (1988), *Understanding Ourselves, The Uses of Therapy*, London, Macmillan.

Based on her work at the Birmingham Women's Counselling and Therapy Centre, the book aims to demystify psychotherapy and the uses it can be put to.

SELF-DEVELOPMENT

These books may help you take a broader approach to some of the problems you can confront as a stepparent.

Stephanie Barrat-Godefroy (1993), *How to Develop Charisma and Personal Magnetism*, London, Thorsons.

Not an immediate thought for stepparents, but this is a fun book aimed at helping you to develop your self-confidence and feel good about yourself.

*Anne Dickson (1982), *A Woman in Your Own Right, Assertiveness and You*, London, Quartet.

Advice, information and exercises to help you develop your assertive self.

*Herbert Fensterheim and Jean Baer (1976), *Don't Say 'Yes' When You Want to Say 'No'*, London, Futura.

Using the authors' own experience, this is a lively assertiveness training book.

Gael Lindenfield (1986), *Assert Yourself: How to reprogramme your mind for positive action*, Northampton, Thorsons.

Simple and accessible. Quick to read and understand.

Linda Tschirhart Sanford and Mary Ellen Donovan (1993), *Women and Self-Esteem: Understanding and improving the way we think and feel about ourselves*, London, Penguin.

Runs to over 400 pages, this is densely packed but well worth dipping into to help you raise your self-esteem.

Liz Willis and Jenny Daisley (1990), *Springboard, Women's Development Workbook*, Stroud, Hawthorn.

Full of exercises and tips, this book is aimed at women who want to make the most of their working life. Includes goal-setting, balancing home and work and finding support. The style is very encouraging and I would say the tips are not just useful for working women, but all women who want to make the most of their lives.

INDEX